D0167031

MATTHEW L. STEVENSON III

CHURCH CLOTHES by Matthew L. Stevenson III

This book or parts thereof may not be reproduced in any form, stored in a retrieval system, or transmitted in any form by any means—electronic, mechanical, photocopy, recording, or otherwise—without prior written permission of the publisher, except as provided by United States of America copyright law.

Unless otherwise noted, all Scripture quotations are taken from the Holy Bible, English Standard Version. Copyright © 2001 by Crossway Bibles, a division of Good News Publishers. Used by permission.

Scripture quotations marked KJV are from the King James Version of the Bible.

Scripture quotations marked NIV are taken from the Holy Bible, New International Version®, NIV®. Copyright © 1973, 1978, 1984, 2011 by Biblica, Inc.® Used by permission of Zondervan. All rights reserved worldwide. www.zondervan.com. The "NIV" and "New International Version" are trademarks registered in the United States Patent and Trademark Office by Biblica, Inc.®

Scripture quotations marked NLT are from the Holy Bible, New Living Translation, copyright © 1996, 2004, 2007. Used by permission of Tyndale House Publishers, Inc., Wheaton, IL 60189. All rights reserved.

Copyright © 2019 by Matthew L. Stevenson III
All rights reserved

Visit the author's website at http://allnationswa.com, http://matthewstevensonworldwide.com.

International Standard Book Number: 978-1-62999-708-7
E-book ISBN: 978-1-62999-711-7

While the author has made every effort to provide accurate internet addresses at the time of publication, neither the publisher nor the author assumes any responsibility for errors or for changes that occur after publication. Further, the publisher does not have any control over and does not assume any responsibility for author or third-party websites or their content.

19 20 21 22 23 — 987654321
Printed in the United States of America

Contents

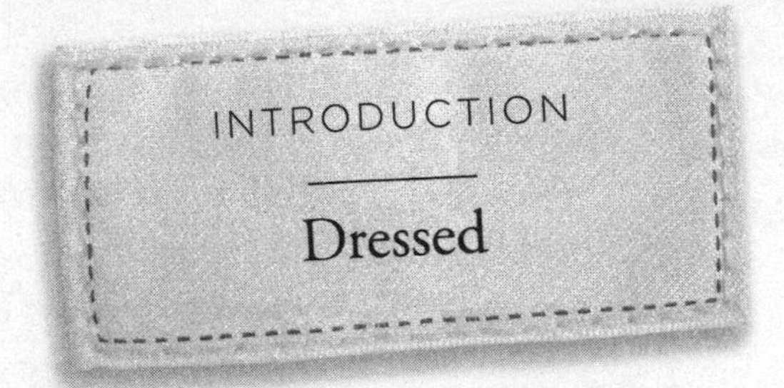

INTRODUCTION

Dressed

CHURCH CLOTHES EQUIPS you with the keys and tools necessary to shift your trajectory and alter your mentality for ministry and life-saving. This in-depth training tool is designed to teach those reading how to take kingdom living to the next level. Our ministry is based on scripturally sound doctrine that you can use as a resource or study guide. As you read this book, be prepared to shift in your mental capacity and obtain nuggets and principles essential to your Christian journey.

As an apostolic voice in the body of Christ, it is imperative that I address certain questions asked regarding what you are about to read.

What qualifies me to lead this discussion?

Why am I a credible voice on this subject matter?

Let me start by introducing myself and explaining what qualifies me to discuss the subject, how my history establishes me as a trusted, credible voice in the body of Christ.

Prior to pastoring, I was a professional in the world of academia. I have degrees in education and taught for several years, developed policies, and consulted in the city's education system. As a consultant I was entrusted to the mayoral board that devoted millions of dollars to turnaround projects. Actually, I continued in education for the first ten years of my pastorate before we went into full-time ministry in 2009. This is why even in my urban characteristic you can hear the philosophical nerd come out. My wife, Kamilah, actually calls me a geek—and quite frankly, I really am a geek. But let's keep that discrete.

Our History

During the early years of our marriage, much of the marital tension Kamilah and I faced was caused by both of our rich educational and professional backgrounds. Kamilah was engulfed in the world of psychology and dedicated twelve years of her professional life to conducting research and counseling families with loved ones diagnosed with Alzheimer's disease. She is a researcher. But in arguments I always held the advantage as an educator. No, seriously. Throughout this book I will reference how our marriage and ministry together has increased our profound knowledge in this subject. Even with our different backgrounds and upbringings, the collaboration of our life has built the principles foundational to *Church Clothes*.

My ministry background began in 1999, when I first started preaching. Primarily being known as a prophetic voice, I was an itinerant minister during conferences, teaching prophetically and on the gifts of the Spirit. I was the prophetic voice for a lot of leaders during this time. That was my strength and earmark before I started our local church. Many people assume my ministry just appeared, but we have been systemically on the rise and gradually building momentum for some time now. When I launched our church, in 2005, I was a single man. In the first year of pastoring I found beauty right in the journey. Later, being joined with my wife, we journeyed through this ministerial call as a team.

We have been very happily married, and neither of us has had an affair. Kamilah has stayed in it, and I have stayed in it—literally all of my adult life. She is older than me but looks younger because she smiles more. We have a powerful marriage and three amazing children. My wife works full-time for me, and I obviously work full-time for her. That is how we do. We love marriage. We love life. We encourage marriage. We counsel marriage. That is what we do.

Currently we both serve in All Nations Worship Assembly. I am the founder, but we both colead and senior lead. We exhibit our leadership in our local church a lot differently. I precede our frontline leaders, which are the first tier of leadership, and subsequently all of the other tiers of leadership. Ultimately I determine the policy, the direction, the vision of the house, and the futuristic oversight. My wife, however, serves in a different capacity.

Kamilah is the pastor over the education department. Our responsibility is to grounding members in the Word of God by transforming them into students at All Nations Worship

Assembly, ensuring that members are informed and applying the things of God in everyday life. Thousands of people have taken our classes.

Our education system is fueled by the diversity in learning and driven by the passion we have for education. Members do not pass classes based on sentimental expertise. Every class in some way encourages people to study. Do I mean members can pass or fail? Or take midterms and finals? Or receive grades and transfers? Yes! We evaluate the standards and protocols of ministry through the educational structure. This is not your little Sunday school procedure; it's a full operation.

In her professional tenure Kamilah is a leadership consultant, coach, and studier of health. For over twenty years my wife has mastered healthy living, weight loss, nutrition consulting, and the study of herbs. Healthy and Better is where she trains on the basic tools needed to attain wholeness in life. She has developed certified course materials in mental, physical, and emotional health. Both of us are passionate about and committed to the wholeness of people.

Now, Kamilah came from a prophetic and deliverance ministry. She traveled with a prophetic theme: prophetic ministry and deliverance. I believe God was training her for a life of ministry and learning the things of God. If you know my wife, you know she literally surrounds herself in the application of godly principles on earth. In our journey, we love ministering to the "outcast." My wife is especially committed to ministering to those bound by pornography, porn stars, people in the streets enjoying gay pride parades, and to the homosexual community. Our ministry reaches people from the love of Jesus. Kamilah wrote one of her first books, *Tough Love—Ministering to the Outcast*, as a result of this journey.

For several years I witnessed my wife minister skillfully to her same gender, those trapped in sex trafficking and prostitution. The most shocking revelation was that most of the people she met on these quests were pastors' kids. That's right—many of the porn stars had church backgrounds. It brought my wife great joy to show the love of God to people rejected by the church. She ministered in clubs and at porn conventions without judging these people. She partied with sinners and won them at the same time.

My wife's ministry was highly supported by unbelievers, by nonbelievers. We saw a lot of people get saved. I remember in one of the prophetic outreaches we began to prophesy over the people in the streets. Even though some of them were visibly inebriated, people received salvation in this setting. Those people followed us to the church after our encounter with them. Our method of ministry was only rejected by the saved people. Zero percent of the backlash was from the world. The most critical comments came from church people.

I remember when my wife started her ministry venture at porn conventions. The number of people, just normal people bound by pornography, was overwhelming. She saw women,

men, and even whole families with children in the actual convention. Someone brought their child in a stroller. It was like a business meeting and people were casually there.

Kamilah posted on Facebook that we were going to minister to porn addicts and stars. The response from people was staggering: "Make sure you bring your Bible. Make sure you sling some oil. Maybe you should bring them out into your environment, but you shouldn't go into theirs." She received several attacks from people within the church and religious communities who felt that Christians should not enter those environments, even to minister. Those environments were off limits to the Christians we encountered.

I am not only a credible source as an apostolic voice but also qualified to address and equip you regarding the areas I have journeyed through. This is a major part of our value system and why Kamilah and I feel so strongly about the unchurched, the de-churched, the outcast, the overlooked, the bored, the unimpressed—all of that—because we spent some time in these ministries.

The premise for this discussion is biblical foundational teaching. I encourage you to grab a notebook because this is a book created to train you.

We named this book *Church Clothes*, but we're not just talking about church clothes. We are talking about the outer workings, the outer manifestation of your faith as a believer, and we're targeting some of those things. We are going to go to the Word of God and try to figure out what the priorities of God are, what is most important to God, and how far we've moved away from that. Hopefully, it is a chance for us to repent and turn from the ways that we thought we would reach the world based on our own opinions and really submit and yield to the Word of God.

CHAPTER 1

The Premise

THE CHURCH IS on God's heart. There is a crisis that must be addressed. The local church is decaying. People are aggressively vacating the church. We have seen media calls for a mass exodus from the church.

As dysfunctional or delayed as people may think the church to be, to call people outside of her is to participate with the schemes and forces of darkness that pull people out of the centrality and the lordship of Jesus Christ. Being a mouthpiece of Christ, I can't sit silently while this is happening. We have to do something, and I believe this is the basis of the "something" we must do.

Is it necessary? Is it the right time? Is it appropriate? Is it even something that deserves attention? My answer to those questions is an emphatic yes! This is the right time. This is the right moment. With the rising deflation of many churches and the discouragement of their leaders, we need to have a clear view about what is contributing to this.

In this book we will dive into some of the pragmatic and

philosophical reasons behind the viewpoints of both people who came up in the church and those who have never been offered an opportunity to truly serve God.

> The Spirit and the Bride say, "Come." And let the one who hears say, "Come." And let the one who is thirsty come; let the one who desires take the water of life without price.
>
> —Revelation 22:17

Filling the house of God with souls must be a priority. This is not just an evangelistic approach. It is both transformational and apostolic in the sense that we should be reversing and reforming a lot of the paradigms that many have both inherited and espoused.

> The Lord is not slow to fulfill his promise as some count slowness, but is patient toward you, not wishing that any should perish, but that all should reach repentance.
>
> —2 Peter 3:9

Many believers in the church have moved away from the priorities of God. The hard truth is that many have been rejected by the church. The church has rejected the world and the outcasts and those who don't look the part because they're not wearing, acting, or doing what the religious think they should. If you have ever experienced this sort of rejection, know that you are always received by the unwavering love of God.

Biblical Premise

In order to effectively address this present crisis, we must address it with the Bible as the premise. I have listed below some key reference points to guide us as we dive deeper into this book:

- I believe that Jesus Christ is the Son of God (John 20:31).
- I believe in salvation, healing, deliverance, and holiness (Rom. 10:9–11; 3 John 2; John 14).
- I believe in hell (Matt. 13:50).
- I believe in sin (1 John 1:9).
- I believe in right and wrong (Rom. 12:9–21).
- I believe in the Word of God, with no exceptions (Heb. 4:12).

This is the premise.

I believe there are a lot of people, leaders, streams, and denominations around the world that believe in the Bible but differ in their beliefs about biblical integrity. The phrase *biblical integrity* is not referring to a man or woman keeping his or her word. Biblical integrity is allowing a person's comprehension, understanding, and ascertaining of the Scriptures to remain true to each scripture's original content, its original context, and its original meaning. Biblical integrity is being extremely compromised in America right now. This is particularly because of the humanist agenda and the antichrist agenda and spirit behind it running through many local churches, leaders, and leadership systems.

We lose biblical integrity by looking at the Word of God through the culture into which we were born. When we approach the Word of God through the lens of our background, we subconsciously make Jesus Christ, who is the Word of God, the mascot for our personal experiences. The Bible was written to and for the human race. The challenges come with the messengers—the ones Paul refers to as "servants of Christ...entrusted with the mysteries God has revealed" (1 Cor. 4:1, NIV). Sometimes in that unlocking we lose things, we tamper with things, and we make things mean what they don't mean. Biblical integrity allows a text to remain true to its original context.

Two concepts involved in the interpretation of Scripture are exegesis and eisegesis. That is the science and the skill of allowing a text to interpret a text. Scripture should interpret Scripture, both in the chapter and in the entire writ of the Word of God, to allow meaning to come forth. That is the process of exegesis.

Eisegesis is taking a scripture, a term, or a phrase out of the chapter, context, and audience—literally out of the hand and the intent of the writer. The Word of God has weight without a person's experience being applied to it, backing it, driving it, or fueling it. We can't afford to have a personal philosophy when it comes to interpreting Scripture. The Scriptures need interpretation by the Spirit that authored it. So that is exegesis and eisegesis, and that's why we have so much confusion about the subject today.

A very simple way to tell the motives of a person who is dissecting Scripture and their interpretation is to consider how close to or how far they fall away from the Great Commandment. One thing I always teach is that if the Word of God, in the way you're interpreting it, makes you love God and people more, then you are on the right track. If it makes you love God and people less, provokes a spirit of fear, causes God to look angry, or draws you away from the nature of God, then you're probably not on the right track.

A part of my assignment to the earth and church is to make sure that the body is aligned with the head. That's a gruesome task. It merits backlash, witchcraft, and accusations. I love Jesus Christ enough to endure that for the sake of the untold millions that could come to the kingdom because somebody wanted to say something. As revivalists we have to bring strong insight to this issue to make sure the unasked questions of this season are given answers that can be found in the Word of God.

I believe that many people's approach to ministry flows from their mentality. Therefore, if a person does not have the right mentality, it will definitely bleed into and affect their approach to ministry. There are a lot of people—thousands of them—who are not being reached because of this limiting, restrictive, erroneous mentality. Asking yourself critical questions regarding your mentality and addressing what needs to be addressed will make you more effective in your ministry.

CHAPTER 2

The Falsehood of Appearance

HERE ARE SOME interesting facts about me that may shock you. I was a traditionalist. I grew up in a traditional church. My family had traditional pastors. I did not believe in women preachers, speaking in tongues, or the gifts of the Spirit. I had supernatural things happen to me my entire life, but I thought those things were common to everyone.

I was also groomed in an environment where I had to wear church clothes. I'm not talking about in a philosophical way. I wore full band collars when I was ordained, clergy tabs when I was licensed, and clergy cords. I could wear only black cords because I wasn't a high-level cleric. I wore them on first Sundays.

I also owned cassocks. I didn't want to wear one, which made me seem like a renegade. I eventually brought the cassock to my church and started wearing it on first Sundays when the preachers had to wear them. I was an extreme traditionalist.

Later, after I married, I crossed over into more of a Charismatic mode of ministry, although I still believed you should never go to church without "church clothes." To me, at that time, it was inappropriate to go to church in jeans or without a tie. I also believed that it was inappropriate to not wear a suit when you preached. I was such a traditionalist that it strained my marriage. Earlier in our marriage, when I was pastoring, my wife would come to church in velour jogging suits. We used to argue about her clothes. I would say, "As the first lady, this is not appropriate," and she would say, "You're not going to change me. I'm not under the same pressure as you." In the midst of me ministering, prophesying, healing, delivering, going to nations, there was a subconscious grooming and pressure that had me feeling that if I didn't dress like this, people were not going to take me seriously; I would not be respected.

I had to come to the reality that God wouldn't penalize me because of what I wore to church. I later came to understand that the posture of my heart was more important than how I was dressed.

My wife didn't grow up in the church. She didn't know the rules. She wasn't taught rules. When she got saved, she didn't try to learn rules. She knew all she needed to know—that God would give her a new heart; her area of study wasn't how to dress. She would often ask me, "Why do you feel like you have to dress like this?" My wife helped me to be free in the Lord instead of feeling like my relationship with Him was contingent upon what I put on or whether or not people will accept me.

One day at church while my wife was worshipping God, a lady came up to her and said, "I see you over there worshipping, but you know, you're going to have to get that piercing out of your eyebrow." My wife did not understand why someone would say that to a twenty-year-old young woman who was worshipping God, loving God, in the house of God. There was no need to point out her appearance. People should work out their own salvation. I'm not saying there aren't times when correction and rebuke are necessary. But my wife was a new believer and new to the church, and she felt ridiculed because she had a piercing. (In Kamilah's defense, she was delivered and freed from a number of things before she removed her eyebrow piercing.)

It is very real the way people will look at you on the outside and not know the transformation that is happening within your heart. I think it is crucial that the church confront this issue and make people aware of this crisis. It's not about what our opinions, experiences, culture, and traditions say; we need to know what the Word of God says about these things.

What is so startling about my wife's experience is that it happened in the 1990s. The fact that we are still talking about this issue, and that it has to be revisited on this scale, is absolutely repulsive. It shows how redundant the religious really are—judging people based on appearance was an issue in the church then, and it is still prevalent today.

The turning point came when Kamilah met a minister of mercy, a strong woman and pioneer named Apostle Jo Ann Long, at church. On her way to meet Jo Ann, Kamilah was stopped halfway down the aisle by a lady who asked her if she was "*saved*

saved." She didn't know who this lady was, but it made Kamilah feel uncomfortable and discouraged because she knew in her heart that she was in one of the greatest places she had ever been in her life with the Lord and wasn't involved in anything negative. When Kamilah made it down the aisle to meet Jo Ann, the apostle complimented her tattoo. She said, "That is a really nice tattoo. I really like that. It's funky." The fact that she engaged my wife and found a way to identify with her opened up Kamilah's heart and allowed her to see that not everyone was judging her based on her outside appearance. It was very comforting for Kamilah to realize that not all Christians were like the people she had met before.

That was a very necessary experience. I believe there is a chance that Kamilah may have backslidden and gone back to her former life had she not met a minister of mercy. This encounter gave her the courage to continue in her pursuit of God and to let Him do whatever He was going to do to perfect her in the way He decided. She realized she did not have to qualify or audition to be accepted in a local church.

Here is what we must realize: The world is moving into the future much faster than the average church is. If we don't learn about appearance and acceptance, we are in trouble. I believe if we don't do something now, the church could be ten to fifteen people meeting in house churches by the time my children are adults. We're here to stop and reverse that, and to make sure the light of God is back on in the house of God.

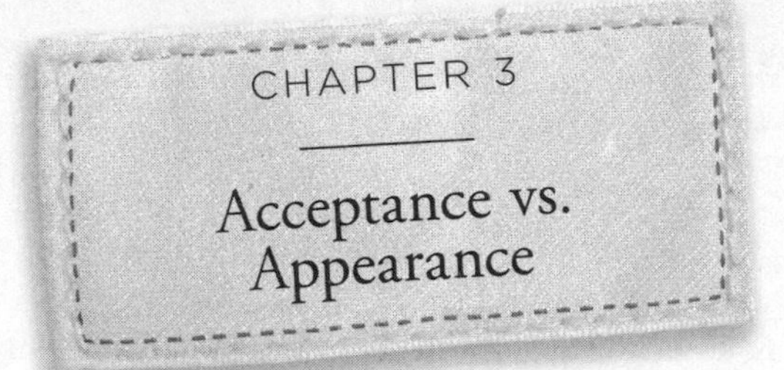

CHAPTER 3

Acceptance vs. Appearance

YOU DO NOT have to strive or perform for God's love. You do not even have to be holy for God to accept you. Holiness should be the aim of every believer, but you do not have to perform in order to attain it. Contrary to popular belief, holiness is not accomplished by the outer workings of the flesh. Acceptance and love from God is something you receive by faith because of the goodness of God.

There are many study habits that contribute to a person's subconscious eisegesis. As I mentioned earlier, in the context of the Bible, eisegesis refers to when you interpret a scripture to mean what you were taught based on your own ideas instead of what it is actually saying. Sometimes what you were taught is not what a scripture means, so I caution you about approaching this teaching or any teaching from an inherited perspective. Revelation pours from the spout of God's mind into the cup of a person's heart. The heart that is going to benefit the most from that pour is the one postured like an unlearned child before the

Lord. Ask Him to teach you to skillfully discern what He meant by what He wrote.

A Lesson on Appearance

> When they came, he looked on Eliab and thought, "Surely the Lord's anointed is before him." But the Lord said to Samuel, "Do not look on his appearance or on the height of his stature, because I have rejected him. For the Lord sees not as man sees: man looks on the outward appearance, but the Lord looks on the heart." Then Jesse called Abinadab and made him pass before Samuel. And he said, "Neither has the Lord chosen this one." Then Jesse made Shammah pass by. And he said, "Neither has the Lord chosen this one." And Jesse made seven of his sons pass before Samuel. And Samuel said to Jesse, "The Lord has not chosen these." Then Samuel said to Jesse, "Are all your sons here?" And he said, "There remains yet the youngest, but behold, he is keeping the sheep." And Samuel said to Jesse, "Send and get him, for we will not sit down till he comes here." And he sent and brought him in. Now he was ruddy and had beautiful eyes and was handsome. And the Lord said, "Arise, anoint him, for this is he." Then Samuel took the horn of oil and anointed him in the midst of his brothers. And the Spirit of the Lord rushed

> upon David from that day forward. And Samuel rose up and went to Ramah.
>
> —1 Samuel 16:6–13

Samuel is my favorite prophet. I could preach about his life, journeys, and ministry forever and never run out of things to say. In this scripture Samuel comes to Jesse's house looking for the next king. At this point, Samuel is the prophet of God. He is the seer. He has access to the future and the people's destiny in his mouth. He knows how to expose the enemy. He is skilled in how to hijack and interrupt the communication channels of the unseen world. He is God's man. Yet even as he approaches Jesse's house, the prophet has no clue about who is going to be installed, authorized, and endorsed as God's man.

Samuel was a man of God who had been groomed in the house of God, and who heard the audible voice of the Lord from the time he was as around eleven years old. Nobody was going to question the words that would come out of the prophet's mouth. That reality is further realized by Samuel's use of the word *surely*, which is a prophetic phrase that means "I guarantee you." This was a test, not just for Jesse and David but also for the prophet Samuel. Why? I believe that part of what God used Samuel to do was extract a people from their present-day culture. Samuel pulled people out of a toxic and delayed culture, because his assignment was the future. He needed to barricade, garrison, and guard the future. God could not use his life as the instrument through which to do that if he did not go to war with the past. This was the past in Samuel's mind. His anointing was the same, and his office was the same, but the past was in his mentality.

When God instructed Samuel not to look on the son's appearance, He knew that Samuel thought for certain, "This is God's man. This is God's dealing. This is God's doing. This is who God has authorized. This is who is going to influence Israel. This is who's going to take Israel to its wars, who's going to redeem it." God said, "Don't look at his appearance," because Samuel had misjudged and thought it was God. He saw the wrong thing and attributed it to God because of where he had been. God said something to Samuel that contradicted Samuel's mentality about appearance, which shows us that the human soul will often subconsciously judge and assess based on appearance.

Corrective Lenses

One of the things that must stop in the body of Christ is the habitual subconscious judging, assessing, and evaluating based on a person's appearance. When appearance allows all of that to happen in your mind and heart, you may miss a powerful opportunity to find out who the Lord's anointed is. God said, "Don't judge his appearance or his height, for I have rejected him," interrupting the prophet's train of thought. Samuel probably would have prophesied and then poured oil on, ordained, and promoted Eliab because he looked how he was supposed to look. His hair looked a certain way. His clothes looked a certain way. He looked good—just gleaming. But God said, "I have rejected him." It is possible to have an acceptable appearance but be rejected by God.

God, who is love and full of mercy, was deliberate about telling His prophet, "Don't look at this man's appearance. I've rejected him." This story unfolds for us a very powerful philosophy: God's eyes and our eyes do not see the same things. The Scripture asks if God were to mark iniquity, who would stand (Ps. 130:3)? If God saw the way men saw, none of us would be able to stand the judgment, measurements, and edicts of God. We have to conceptualize that God does not see the way we were brought up. We see through the lens of our upbringing, specifically through three lenses: the lens of tradition, the lens of preference, and the lens of culture. Our lenses, interactions, determinations, judgments, and sometimes our accusations are based on tradition, culture, and preference.

People—including many pastors, leaders, and bloggers—often think that God sees things the way they see them, like God is obligated to agree with them, and there is no agreement in that. God is not an external God. People judge by outward appearance, but the Lord looks at the heart.

The devastating principle is that the reason why the church is dying and losing members—losing the homosexual community, gang rappers, and even entrepreneurs, particularly those in the inner-city African American church—is because we are not heart readers. We have no ability to weigh, decipher, or discern what God is doing in people.

A Deeper Look

God looks at the heart. If salvation, sanctification, and holiness begin after hearing the heart of a man, then our inability to see the heart is the barrier keeping us from reaching it. We are external people who build a cosmetic Christianity, who force people to live up to our outward standards, as if God is an outward God.

Back to the story in 1 Samuel 16, this was an entire cycle of selection. They were probably there for hours trying to figure out who was going to be the one to take the nation to the future, who deserved to be the king and have influence. Eventually Samuel had to ask Jesse, "Are these all the sons that you have?" There are sons out there who are being overlooked and misjudged because their appearance is stopping our reach to them. Beware if the extent of your revelation regarding a person is limited by how you see him or her at first glance.

Your churches would be filled if you could take a deeper look. Your messages would actually have some weight if you would take a deeper look. Our evangelism, discipleship, and counseling would be more effective if we would take a deeper look. I believe the Lord is looking in your church and saying, "Are these all the sons you have?" Looking at your businesses, asking, "Are these all the sons you have?" Looking through your manuscripts and your projects and asking, "Are these all the sons you have?" Is your only appeal to those who look the way you think they should look?

After Samuel had gone through all of Jesse's sons, almost as an afterthought Jesse remembered David was out in the fields. The son that had been forgotten because of his appearance was the one the Lord wanted to anoint! Sometimes God anoints those who look opposite from what we are willing to accept, promote, platform, or follow.

Stumbling Over Appearance

What is even more profound about this entire ordeal is that you see this type of ideology contrasted even between the Jews and the Gentiles. The Jews were viewed as the righteous ones based on their appearance, while the Gentiles were condemned solely based on their "unapproved" appearance.

> What shall we say, then? That Gentiles who did not pursue righteousness have attained it, that is, a righteousness that is by faith; but that Israel who pursued a law that would lead to righteousness did not succeed in reaching that law. Why? Because they did not pursue it by faith, but as if it were based on works. They have stumbled over the stumbling stone, as it is written, "Behold, I am laying in Zion a stone

> of stumbling, and a rock of offense; and whoever believes in him will not be put to shame."
>
> —Romans 9:30–33

The Jews were the ones who appeared to be righteous—who pursued the law, who kept the law, and who quoted the Torah. However, Scripture says they did not obtain their goal. Why not? They pursued it not by faith, but by works.

What's so bad about this is that we put to shame those who don't have the appearance that we want them to have, but in the Scripture it says that the Jews, who had the appearance of righteousness, actually didn't attain it. The ones who were not even in pursuit of righteousness did attain it because they pursued it by faith. We have to now restructure what our principles and what our theology is on people and their acceptance. Who has a relationship with God? Who is accepted? Who is received by God? We can't just base that upon appearance, because here the Scripture says that the ones who we would have thought had the appearance of righteousness didn't receive it because they stumbled over it.

There are certain leaders out there who, because of their people group and the leaders that they're with, are afraid to launch out and do the right thing. The right thing is to accept people and stand up for people who have been rejected.

Again we see this issue addressed in the conflict between the apostles Peter and Paul. Peter was a Jew. Peter believed in the law. He understood the law. He abided by the law. But then here comes Paul preaching a different gospel. (Even though Paul was also a Jew, his apostolic commission changed the standard by which he lived.)

> As he does in all his letters when he speaks in them of these matters. There are some things in them that are hard to understand, which the ignorant and unstable twist to their own destruction, as they do the other Scriptures.
>
> —2 Peter 3:16

Peter was basically saying this gospel was different from the one they had been living. The "gospel" of the Jews was that you had to follow the law precisely! As Paul begins to give this different gospel, Peter says, "It's a hard gospel to comprehend; nevertheless, it is the Word of God. But your heart can be blinded by it, and you'll stumble in destruction because you can't receive what God is saying."

Although he knew that Paul was preaching the gospel, Peter comes under the fear of man when the other Jews come into town. It causes him to operate in hypocrisy, even as a leader, even as one knowing what the truth is.

> But when Cephas came to Antioch, I opposed him to his face, because he stood condemned. For before certain men came from James, he was eating with the Gentiles; but when they came he drew back and

> separated himself, fearing the circumcision party. And the rest of the Jews acted hypocritically along with him, so that even Barnabas was led astray by their hypocrisy. But when I saw that their conduct was not in step with the truth of the gospel, I said to Cephas before them all, "If you, though a Jew, live like a Gentile and not like a Jew, how can you force the Gentiles to live like Jews?" We ourselves are Jews by birth and not Gentile sinners; yet we know that a person is not justified by works of the law but through faith in Jesus Christ, so we also have believed in Christ Jesus, in order to be justified by faith in Christ and not by works of the law, because by works of the law no one will be justified.
>
> —Galatians 2:11–16

According to their religion, the Jews weren't supposed to be eating with the Gentiles, much less eating what they eat! Peter had received the message. He understood. He had even eaten with the Gentiles. But now, when he gets around his other buddies who still believe the old message, he becomes a hypocrite.

This is a message to leaders. It is imperative that leaders remember that leadership can be a skill you develop, but it is also a grace gift of the Spirit. When you have the grace of leadership, you are leading people whether you want to or not. Paul harshly rebuked Peter for his hypocrisy, because when leaders judge based on appearance it becomes a matter of bad stewardship.

Leaders, please do not waste the grace of God on your life by leading others into hypocrisy because somebody doesn't meet your personal standard of appearance. Every man can be accepted by God, and it has nothing to do with appearance—the real standard is, what do you believe?

CHAPTER 4

The Right Standard

THE CHURCH WORLD has an upside-down way of thinking when it comes to people's salvation, particularly if they are accepted by God or able to receive the other blessings the Lord promises us in the Scriptures. We have to move away from thinking that we have to perform to receive these things from Christ and put our faith in Jesus. The church has made a group of people operate according to a standard in order to be accepted and received by God. However, that was never God's intent!

Why did Jesus come to the earth? What was the purpose? Why did Jesus die on the cross?

> Many of the Jews therefore, who had come with Mary and had seen what he did, believed in him, but some of them went to the Pharisees and told them what Jesus had done. So the chief priests and the Pharisees gathered the council and said, "What are we to do? For this man performs many signs. If we

> let him go on like this, everyone will believe in him, and the Romans will come and take away both our place and our nation." But one of them, Caiaphas, who was high priest that year, said to them, "You know nothing at all. Nor do you understand that it is better for you that one man should die for the people, not that the whole nation should perish." He did not say this of his own accord, but being high priest that year he prophesied that Jesus would die for the nation, and not for the nation only, but also to gather into one the children of God who are scattered abroad. So from that day on they made plans to put him to death.
>
> —John 11:45–53

Jesus died on the cross to bring the scattered children back and to form a new creation in Christ. When the Bible talks about how old things have passed away and all things have become new, it is talking about a new creation.

> Therefore, if anyone is in Christ, he is a new creation. The old has passed away; behold, the new has come. All this is from God, who through Christ reconciled us to himself and gave us the ministry of reconciliation; that is, in Christ God was reconciling the world to himself, not counting their trespasses against them, and entrusting to us the message of reconciliation. Therefore, we are ambassadors for Christ, God

> making his appeal through us. We implore you on behalf of Christ, be reconciled to God.
>
> —2 Corinthians 5:17–20

> For he himself is our peace, who has made us both one and has broken down in his flesh the dividing wall of hostility by abolishing the law of commandments expressed in ordinances, that he might create in himself one new man in place of the two, so making peace, and might reconcile us both to God in one body through the cross, thereby killing the hostility. And he came and preached peace to you who were far off and peace to those who were near. For through him we both have access in one Spirit to the Father.
>
> —Ephesians 2:14–18

Making people's appearance a prerequisite for acceptance creates a dividing wall of hostility and goes against the purpose for which Jesus died on the cross. He died on the cross so that He could bring a new creation and we could all have access to Him by the same Spirit. It's not by any man's performance or work. That mode of thinking and behavior was not even advantageous in the Old Testament.

God wants the wall of hostility to come down. When we continue to make people strive to look a certain way before they feel accepted, we create a barrier that keeps them from getting to

God. These same people are the ones that need God. This is a crucial issue because, again, it goes against the very reason why Jesus died on the cross. The crux of Jesus' mission was to bring us together in a sense of unity and oneness.

Defining Tradition

It is imperative that we understand the power of tradition as it relates to the course correction we are on regarding appearance and acceptance. A tradition is basically a practiced value that is done or rehearsed continually. Something becomes important—a representation of something—we repeat it, and then it becomes sacred to us. Traditions are not necessarily born sacred but are actions done so frequently and so reverently over time that they become what we call traditions.

Here is a fundamental fact about tradition: it is not bad. I am a Charismatic minister. I prophesy. I do spiritual warfare. I minister deliverance. But I probably know more hymns than most of you reading this book! I sing old songs. I believe in hymns. My great-grandmother traveled with the Caravans and James Cleveland. So I understand tradition.

Traditions are not evil. Every race, city, and family has them. They grow and ferment to become wicked when they become gods that demand your worship. Because a tradition is narrow, it is sacred. You protect it. Often there is a tendency to become idolatrous over a tradition. There is a subtle difference between tradition and traditionalism. You have grown into traditionalism when your tradition makes you devalue or misdefine another human being or their story.

Traditionalism is the seed of arrogance, anger, and pride that belittles, abuses, and demeans those who don't share the same tradition. Jesus was born into a succession of traditions. He studied them. He understood them. He debated them. And yet when it came to addressing tradition, He said they "[made] void the word of God by your tradition that you have handed down" (Mark 7:13). The danger of traditionalism is that it can dull the Word of God. Jesus, who is the Word, taught His followers that we compromise the effectiveness, accuracy, and impact of the Word of God because of our traditions. If the Word said that about the Word, it is something every believer should take to heart.

Traditionalism is dangerous. It is not dangerous to have a tradition; it is dangerous to use your tradition as the basis for your judgment or your acceptance of other people. You take away weight from the eternal Word because of your tradition.

Some people dress a certain way as a matter of tradition. I don't judge you. If I were to judge you for dressing traditionally, I would be equally wicked as those who judge others for *not* dressing traditionally. I don't have a problem with garments; I know some anointed preachers who prefer them because of the symbolism behind them, and that is their particular value system. I don't think this makes them less or more than anyone else, but dressing in traditional garments doesn't make you more refined or sophisticated, and unfortunately, it does not give you authority. Your appearance does not contribute to how you are viewed in the unseen world. It contributes to how audiences respond or receive you.

Defining Culture

When traditions are passed down, a culture is developed. Culture can be obvious and invisible. Culture determines the policy by which people gather and operate. When it is a toxic culture, it's like carbon monoxide; it's invisible, and when it grows, it kills everybody. Culture represents the tapestry that develops our language, dialect, and what is important to us. Some people grew up in a culture of affirmation. All Nations Worship Assembly is a very affectionate church. It is a part of our tapestry as a deliverance people.

As a matter of culture, people dress a certain way. The Romans dressed a certain way. The Greeks dressed a certain way. The Hebrews dressed a certain way. Every race and background brings a culture to the table. The challenge comes in when we try to make our culture the culture of the kingdom. We act like the kingdom is our culture because that's what bred us and contributed to our victory. Our culture is crafted by how we grew up and how we were trained. The schematics of our academics provided what became important to us. It's culture, the way we do a thing. A tradition may be what we do, but culture is the way we do it.

I once preached in the oldest Baptist church in the Bahamas.

As a Baptist boy myself, I understood the culture. I was not offended, thrown off, or distracted by the culture. I understood it. I was sitting next to the father of Dr. Myles Munroe, in the middle of talking, when hymn time came. I stood with the rest of the congregation to go and sing the hymn. My wife remained seated. She did not understand the culture. She had no idea what was going on. When we later discussed this incident, Kamilah explained to me that as they kept signaling for her to come to the front, she was thinking, "I don't want to go up there." Kamilah later realized that it was offensive, not intentionally, but because she had no clue what was going on in that culture.

There are certain people who appear a certain way because of culture. Baptist people have things that they do. Pentecostal people have things that they do. Methodist people have things that they do. Prior to starting my church, I was part of an Assemblies of God church, and even we had a culture. Every group of people develops over time a culture or a behavior pattern that determines what they wear and how they look at people who wear things different from them. It is important to realize that your particular culture does not put a restriction or refinement on God or His house.

Defining Preference

There are things that we prefer based on tradition or our culture. If you preach, wear a tie. When I was growing up, if you were going to take Communion, you had to wear something white.

On Mother's Day in my church, if your mother was alive you wore red roses; if your mother was deceased, you wore white roses. These were cultural things. They were not scripted anywhere. You couldn't find them logged anywhere. All of these things exclusively reflect preferences: "When I go to church, I prefer for this to happen."

Preferences are personal desires, affinities, and things that we just respond well to. If something is not in line with our preference, we often disrespect it. Generally, the human heart is full of self-centeredness. It is actually the essence and mentality that drives the sin nature. It's self-worship. Preference is a form of that, especially when we are imprisoned by our preferences.

As a boy, when it was cold outside—and there is no cold like Chicago cold—I would wear hats. When my hair was lower, I would wear hats. I would wear hats in churches because often many of the churches I was a part of couldn't pay their bills, so it would still be cold inside the building. I would come in, as they were trying to raise money for heaters or whatever was going on, and I would come in with my hat on and maybe sit at the back of the church.

One time, a mother wearing a very elaborate hat (I'll never forget it—it was mint green with a veil that covered half the woman's face like Moses and some wheat things coming out of it) approached me. She informed me that it was disrespectful, dishonorable, and irreverent for me to wear my hat in the sanctuary. She went on further to say that when you come into the sanctuary, it is polite for you to take your hat off. Now this is a typical "church clothes" discussion. In my ignorance I wondered, "What is the difference between my hat and your hat? If God is mad at me or can't see my thoughts or thinks I'm in rebellion because I have on a Bulls hat, certainly He should be offended by your peacock hat. He should be mad that you've taken the sheaves from the harvest fields and put them on your head. What makes it even worse is that you probably went into debt to do so!"

This has now become a game of semantics. Some hats are appropriate. Some hats are not appropriate. Who's right? The real truth is, nobody. Everybody's wrong, because God is not stumbling over whether you wear a hat inside of that building. If God is stumbling over you wearing a hat in the building, He's also stumbling over you wearing a hat in your car, because God is omniscient. He doesn't change His attitude. He said in the Book of Malachi, "I change not" (3:6, KJV). He doesn't change His attitude or desire for you when you go into the house or the car, so if wearing a hat in church is wicked, it should be wicked to wear a hat at home or anywhere else. Take your hats off everywhere. That is a church clothes stronghold. Church hats are acceptable, but don't wear a skullcap. It's disrespectful. We could argue all day about what God feels disrespected by, but I doubt He is mad about your skullcap. That's an issue of preference.

We have just defined tradition, culture, and preference. There are people who have a preference. "Don't wear that here." When my wife went to minister at a cultural church a few years ago, she wore a skirt. She did not walk in there with some gym shoes on, although I'm sure she would much rather have done that. She didn't walk in there with a jersey on. She wore her suit. Why? When in Rome, do as the Romans do. Paul became all things to all men so that he might win some. (See 1 Corinthians 9:19–23.)

When I'm preaching in a church or in a setting where I know the congregation will receive a person better if he dresses a certain way, I'm going to dress according to what the people want so they will receive the words coming out of my mouth. I'm not going to walk in and deliberately be countercultural to the environment. Depending upon the assignment, I may be coming to address, correct, restore, heal, rebuke, or judge—but I don't want what I wear to be a distraction. However, when I'm on my own, doing my own thing, I'm going to wear what I want to wear. That's preference.

Here is the danger: when tradition, culture, or preference becomes treated as doctrine, it becomes demonic. Paul warned us about the doctrines of demons. I believe there is a species and a category of demonic spirits who are intellectual and cerebral in nature. They gather scriptures that Christians mishandle and use them to beat the broken, keep the backslidden in that state, or push the lost soul away from the cross. It makes the church unattractive.

Colossians 2:8 talks about not being robbed and spoiled by the philosophies of man, by deceptive philosophies that come from human tradition. These preferences and traditions rob you of your ability to have real access to God.

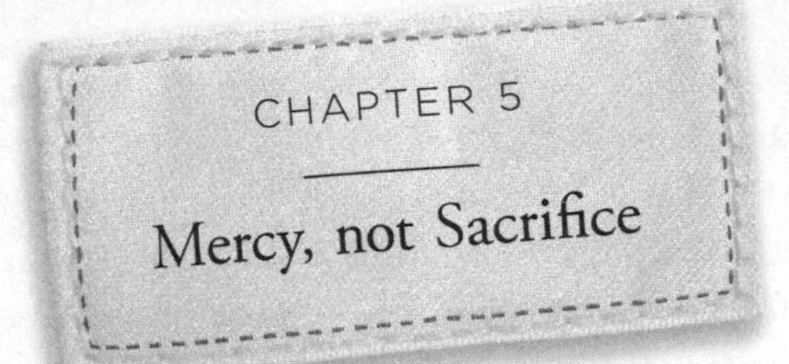

CHAPTER 5

Mercy, not Sacrifice

One of the things that I liken appearance to—you have to dress a certain way, you have to look a certain way—is a level of sacrifice, which again is OK if you want to sacrifice to that level. If you say, "Hey, I'm going to put my best clothes on. I'm going to make sure I'm good from head to toe. I've got my hat." That's all great. The sacrifice is great.

However, what I liken acceptance to is mercy, which means irrespective if you have the appearance, we're still going to accept you. I want to point out some scriptures to help you understand what God thinks about sacrifice versus mercy.

> For I desire mercy, not sacrifice, an acknowledgement of God rather than burnt offering.
>
> —Hosea 6:6

In Matthew 9:9–13, as Jesus is partying with Matthew the tax collector, first of all He tells him, "Come, follow Me." He's sitting down, eating at the dinner table. I'm sure He's partying, because Matthew was a tax collector, and trust me, if He was speaking in tongues, the Pharisees wouldn't have had anything to say. He tells Matthew, "Come, follow Me." And He goes and He kicks it with Matthew. To the Jews, Matthew was worse than a sinner. There were sinners, and then there were tax collectors. These were traitors to their own country. These were the worst kind. Some of the disciples, they were sinners, but they weren't tax collectors. People started whispering, "Why is your teacher sitting with a tax collector?" He looked over at them and He said, "Go and learn what this means," meaning that this was something they had to learn. That's interesting, because they were well learned in the law. They were well learned in the Ten Commandments and the Torah, but there was obviously something that they had not learned, so He tells them, "Go and learn what this means. I desire mercy over a sacrifice." They couldn't get it.

Psalm 50:7–13 shows us what God thinks about sacrifice: "Listen, my people, and I will speak; I will testify against you, Israel: I am God, your God. I bring no charges against you concerning your sacrifices...which are ever before me" (vv. 7–8, NIV). God is saying He is not going to rebuke us over our sacrifice; basically, "That's fine. You can have your sacrifice. I will not rebuke you." He continues, "I have no need of a bull from your stall or of goats from your pens, for every animal of the forest is mine, and the cattle on a thousand hills"—which a lot of people use as a money scripture, but I'm using it here to prove a different point—"I know every bird in the mountains and the insects in the fields are mine. If I were hungry I would not tell you, for the world is mine, and all that is in it. Do I eat the flesh of bulls or drink the blood of goats?" (vv. 9–13, NIV).

In Deuteronomy 32 God talked about how other gods eat the fat of the offering, but what He's saying is, "Listen, I don't necessarily need your sacrifice. Your sacrifice is your language, is your communication. And guess what? I'll accept it, because that's the way that you're proving to Me that you love Me. But it's not proving how much I love you or how I'm going to accept you." So He says, "I'm not going to rebuke you for it, but I don't have a need for it. The sacrifice is something you're doing for Me, because it's posturing your heart in a certain way, but it's not posturing My heart in a certain way." The problem is not the sacrifice; the problem is when we don't understand mercy over the sacrifice, and when we make God contingent, as if someone who sacrifices more is going to get more acceptance from God.

I also want to point out a few other scriptures to establish what was important to God. If the sacrifice is not important and He desires mercy over the sacrifice, then what is it that God is after? What is it that He deems more important than the sacrifice? What is this mercy He wants us to learn about?

In Isaiah 1 God refers to Israel as Sodom and Gomorrah. This is interesting. Let me tell you what the sin problem was with Sodom and Gomorrah. Isaiah 1:10–11 says, "Hear the word of the LORD, you rulers of Sodom; listen to the instruction of our

God, you people of Gomorrah! 'The multitude of your sacrifices—what are they to me?' says the Lord. 'I have more than enough of burnt offerings, of rams and the fat of fattened animals; I have no pleasure in the blood of bulls and lambs and goats'" (NIV). These were pagan sacrifices; but I'm just establishing how God really feels about the sacrifice. In verse 17 He basically says, "Listen, I want you to learn to do right. I want you to seek justice. I want you to defend the oppressed, take up the cause of the fatherless, and plead the case of the widow."

What were the sins of Sodom? Ezekiel 16:49 tells us: "Now this was the sin of your sister Sodom: She and her daughters were arrogant, overfed, and unconcerned; they did not help the poor and needy" (NIV).

Here is the thing. We are trying to do everything to get our relationship right with God. We are trying to get people to perform, to look the part, to do this, to do that, to try to get the acceptance from God and from the church, while Jesus is saying, "I really don't care about the sacrifice. I'm not going to rebuke it; I'll let you do it. But how about this? Make sure that your priorities are right. I would much rather you feed the homeless, give shelter to those who have no shelter, see about those who are sick, establish justice, and help the hopeless."

God has told us what His priorities are, and we are still fighting over making people look the part to feel accepted by the church. Who are we to judge, when Jesus has already accepted them? What we're supposed to be doing is breaking down that wall, that division of hostility. We are supposed to be coming together as one to minister, not counting faults or sins but receiving people, lending them mercy, and giving hope to those who have no hope.

We think that because we go to church, because we're fasting, because we're praying, God will accept us more. No, He won't—especially if we don't show mercy. There are people who have hostility and hatred in their hearts. They are so judgmental, it's not even funny. They reject people based upon how they look. And they think God is going to receive their offerings. Why? Because they think, "If I put the blood on the altar, I'm all good. I can still talk about people. I can still reject them. I can still push them away and make them feel unwanted. I can continue to push the outcast out even further because I put the blood on the altar and I go to church and I fast." I'm not saying there's anything wrong with bringing God a sacrifice, going to church, or fasting. Actually, there are some reasons why we should do these things. What I'm saying is that if you feel like you have to give people a standard to live up to or tell them to look a certain way, or you can't wear this outfit, or you can't wear this hair color, or you can't do this because these are my opinions of it, you have misunderstood God.

I wanted to point out Scripture concerning the sacrifice to establish that Jesus never asked for our sacrifice. What He did require was mercy, and that was throughout the Old and the New Testaments.

CHAPTER 6

Hypocrisy and Cosmetic Christianity

We're still dealing with appearance, and now we're going to look at some principles, and then I'm going to let you know something about acceptance. To illustrate these concepts we will look at Jesus' words to the Pharisees found in Matthew 23:25–34.

Jesus begins, "What sorrow awaits you teachers of religious law and you Pharisees. Hypocrites!" (v. 25, NLT). Hypocrisy is the spirit primarily responsible for a lot of what I call "cosmetic Christianity." He says, "You are so careful"—people put a great amount of effort into this—"to clean the outside of the cup and the dish" (v. 25, NLT). He uses the cup and the dish as illustrations because they are items used for serving and the Pharisees wanted people to receive from them. They were so eager, so effortful, so laborious, so stressed out under the pressure of externalized Christianity that they "clean the outside of the cup and the dish, but inside [they] are filthy—full of greed and self-indulgence! You blind Pharisee!" What did we learn earlier in the prophet Samuel's case? God taught him that we don't see things the way God does, and in order for Samuel to take God's people where He wanted them to go, God had to remove the blinders off the prophet.

Jesus continues in verse 26, "First wash the inside of the cup and the dish, and then the outside will become clean, too" (NLT). I wish you would get that. That is an appearance and an acceptance scripture. The washing begins within. It does not begin with hair. Here is a problem. People say, "If you wear jeans and I like how they fit you, then I will start looking at you." Madam, that's a personal problem. It has nothing to do with what is presented before you. Jesus is talking about internal cleansing. Once we are clean on the inside, the outside will become clean too.

If you get distracted by the appearance of a choir person or singer or a dancer and it irritates you, it may not be a spiritual thing at all. Maybe you're just too easily distracted. We can't spiritualize our assessments of things because of our inability to be disciplined under the Word of God. If Barney came and told you to repent or delivered the word from the Lord, would you receive from him? Most of you wouldn't, because it's Barney, and we need to realize that's not Barney's problem. It's yours.

Look at verse 27: "What sorrow awaits you teachers of religious law and you Pharisees. Hypocrites!" (NLT). Again Jesus is dealing with hypocrisy. Jesus was consistent in dealing with hypocrisy. "For you are like whitewashed tombs" (v. 27, NLT). Look at the phrase "whitewashed tombs." In biblical times, tombs did not have to be whitewashed. Jesus was blasting the effort that people go through to make sure they look the way people want them to look. A whitewashed tomb was actually a tomb or mausoleum given to a person who was affluent, who came from an affluent family, and who had been prepared for death. They would literally paint the tombs white to make sure that when people walked past the tomb, they would know that this was an affluent man, a prepared person; this was a member of the social elite, a high-class person. This person was whitewashed.

By calling the religious teachers of His day "whitewashed tombs," Jesus was saying they were beautiful on the outside but on the inside they were filled not with the Holy Ghost but with dead people's bones. Hmm. I thought about that. The only way to become filled with the bones of a human is to consume them, to be a carnivore, an eater of people, somebody who bites and devours. The only way you could get dead men's bones in you is by swallowing them. You took them hostage. You made them as your own and hid them. Jesus said they were "filled on the inside with dead people's bones and all sorts of impurity" (v. 27, NLT). He is messing with their ideas that externally acceptable, externally preferential, externally whatever doesn't always mean holy, doesn't always mean pure—doesn't always mean anything.

Again, this is an appearance issue. Jesus warned the apostles in Matthew 10:16 that they were being sent out as sheep among wolves, but He also counseled them in Matthew 7:15 to beware of wolves in sheep's clothing. We need to be careful not to receive, regard, respect, revere, welcome, and promote a wolf just because he is wearing a sheep coat. I think that is what we've done, which is why we have molesters, pedophiles, and predatory behavior in the church. A lot of our selections are wolflike; they just know how to put on the sheep's stuff.

Jesus continues in verse 28, "You look like righteous people" (NLT). Outwardly the Pharisees looked like righteous people, which means—drumroll, please—righteousness does have a look, or so they thought, preached, or believed. "You look like righteous people, but inwardly your hearts are filled with hypocrisy and lawlessness" (v. 28, NLT). That is a strong statement from Jesus.

Jesus continues in verse 29, "What sorrow awaits you teachers of religious law and you Pharisees. Hypocrites! For you build tombs for the prophets your ancestors killed" (NLT). In other words, you talk about the forefathers and coming up in holiness, about being reared by the mothers of old and the deacons of old and the fathers of old. You're talking. You build tombs for them and decorate the monuments of the godly people your ancestors actually destroyed. "Then you say, 'If we had lived in the days of our ancestors, we would never have joined them in killing the prophets'" (v. 30, NLT). Prophets need to be prepared for the response when we present truth like this. Whenever a prophetic voice addresses the system and those who are victims and sons of it, a murderous, angry spirit comes out.

Look at verse 31. This is going to fascinate you. Look at what He says: "But in saying that, you testify against yourselves that you are indeed the descendants of those who murdered the prophets" (NLT). This means that the religious spirit cannot coexist with the prophetic spirit. You cannot be legitimately prophetic and have the religious spirit. Once a prophet—or a hopeful, would-be, or pretend-to-be—becomes an advocate of any one preference, culture, or stream, he or she has ceased to speak for God. You have murdered the prophets. Teachers of religious law murdered the prophetic anointing.

This is what verse 32 says: "Go ahead and finish what your ancestors started" (NLT). I love this Jesus. He continues: "Snakes! Sons of vipers!" (v. 33, NLT). Your mom is a viper, and your daddy is a viper. You are the way you are because of how you were raised. You are the way you are because a reptile spirit raised you. It taught you to bite and wrap yourself around people because they look like prey, like victims. "How will you escape the judgment of hell?" (v. 33, NLT).

Finally, here's what blesses me: verse 34. Look at what Jesus had the nerve to say to these wolves He has been talking about in verses 25–33: "Therefore, I am sending you prophets" (v. 34, NLT). His prophets would have the ability to peer past the external and know what the Pharisees were doing internally. Jesus was going to send these "prophets and wise men and teachers of religious law. But you will kill some by crucifixion, and you will flog others with whips in your synagogues [churches], chasing them from city to city" (v. 34, NLT).

What does that spirit do today? Blog, write, video, get your natural oils in your face, get on and bash. That is the same spirit that tries to drive out a prophetic word from city to city, from church to church. It tries to flog the prophet, even kill him or her, because it doesn't like the alarm, the sound that comes with a prophetic word that deals with cosmetic Christianity.

Meditate on the tension points in Matthew 23:25–34. Is your way, your approach, focused on the external? I don't think anybody is right or wrong. I couldn't care less. Unfortunately—and I may get criticized for saying this, but I say it in humility and the love of God—African American people have a tendency to get distracted by this external stuff. Inner city, traditional, tambourine beating—we are the only people that do that. If you go to some of our Caucasian streams, they don't care. These are not priorities to them.

I'm not saying that we should try to mimic or be like anyone else. It's just unfortunate that as a people African Americans have been so robbed of their right to be internally integral that we put everything on display. I mean, you know when a black person wins the lottery, don't you? You know when a black person is getting ready to hit tax time because we immediately go and buy a zoot suit, we change our hair—we do whatever we need to do to show you we're rich. We get spinners on our cars. And listen, we won't pay off mortgages. We won't save, because most African American kids either can't go to college or will have to go to college on their own bill, and whoever went before them didn't save, so we're not going to set up for the future. We have to set up

GoFundMe pages to pay for funerals. Most of us don't have life insurance. But when we get the first piece of money, we're going to do external things, aren't we?

Not everyone is like that. We know millionaires who wear polos and shop at Sears. What am I saying?

There are people who are not in the faith who we look at and judge because they're not in church or they don't live up to our expectations who are better mothers, better fathers, better wives, and better husbands. They take care of their kids. They steward their money well. They're humanitarians. They feed the poor. They help the sick. They show mercy. This is why we have to be careful not to judge or reject these types of people, because in God's eyes they are actually doing what Jesus told the church to do. We're no better than them if we sit and judge them because they're not living up to our expectations.

I know some very hateful, mean, hostility-in-their-hearts-type people in the church who think they are holy because they do a bunch of religious acts. Again, I'm not discounting sacrifice. It is a great thing. God accepts it. However, it is not what God has asked us to do.

God has asked us to go out into the world to compel people to come in, to reach the lost, to feed the hungry. There are some things that we need to start doing that we're not doing. We are supposed to be accepting of the world, to bring them into the fold. It's quite interesting, and I tell people all the time, that I know some really solid people who are not believers and they act sweeter than a lot of churchgoing people.

This is contributing to the decay of the African American church. We are so external. I think that same externalism is why we won't get counseling, we won't get therapy, and we won't admit when we've been raped, molested, or touched. We won't admit to an addiction; we just call it an "issue." We won't admit that it is dysfunctional for Grandmother to sleep in one room and Granddaddy to sleep in the other one. We won't admit that it's dysfunctional for people's sisters to also be their cousins. We won't admit any of that stuff. We won't admit any of it, because we are an external people, and because of what we've been through, because of what we've faced in life, we are forced to put it on, make it all look OK on the outside. I could be beating the stew out of you right now, but to put it on I'm going to force you to be cosmetic, make it look OK. What goes on in the house of God is often the same mentality that operates through poverty and a very strong religious spirit in people. This is a real challenge.

What do terrorism groups, gangs, the homosexual community, and the porn industry have in common? They're not afraid of acceptance. You could actually be recruited—they have gay families—be accepted, and unfortunately, it mimics biblical discipleship.

Most gangbangers are in gangs because of the acceptance. They feel like their gang is a family. If you pull somebody out of one family, you have to put them back in another family. The problem is that the church pulls them out and then we try to get them to look a certain way before they feel accepted. If they're coming out of acceptance, if we're going to win them, we have to bring them into a family.

That is why many gangsters don't come out. Unless something changes, they're not going to come out. This is why that spirit of sexual perversion, that spirit of drug addiction is going to stay. They're coming from community to chaos. They're coming from places where nobody judges them and everybody accepts them; they're coming out of that.

Nobody wants to be in an environment of rejection.

But here's the thing. If we don't learn acceptance in the church, we will continue to fail the homosexual community. We're going to fail the former thug, the former gangster. We're going to fail a lot of people because we are afraid of acceptance. I know a lot of people are afraid of hearing, "I cannot accept you. I can't hug you. I can't embrace you. I can't be seen around you. I can't pray for you, because if I do, that means I agree with you."

If we're friends of sinners, then we get persecuted. The church will persecute us if we become friends to sinners and accept sinners into our world, into our space, into our culture. God forbid we get attacked by the church. There are a lot of people that we accept that we don't agree with.

I accept a lot of people. That is the problem many people have with collaboration and partnerships between the sacred and secular. We don't understand acceptance. We don't understand that you can think people are important and not agree with who they are or what they have to say. It doesn't matter. A part of the brilliance of the way we do church at our church, All Nations, is acceptance, and that is a catalyst for deliverance. No, we don't agree. Yes, we disagree. No, we don't think that this is right. Yes, if you don't come to Christ, you will go to hell. But we're going to accept you. We're going to show you we accept you, because acceptance opens the human heart. You can say whatever you want when you accept a person.

Many people don't want to come to church because church people are mean. Let's just be honest. Church people are mean. They're grossly mean. They will talk about you if your life is not up to par with where they think your life is supposed to be. If you accept someone, if you collaborate with someone, all of a sudden you become an outcast because church people don't agree with it. Here you have Jesus, who died for all man's sins. He is married to the backslider. He is a friend of sinners.

But do you think the church is effective with backsliders? Absolutely not, because they're not like us. If we were, there wouldn't be storefronts. This is the reason the law had to come down, not because it was going to judge us, but because of the hostility. The wall of division is what it goes back to. Actually, in God's heart the law is based off of the Great Commandment, which is to love God and to love people. All the laws and the prophets hinge on that, so I think the church has to reprioritize the way we view some of these things. Our actions should be a display of love, acceptance, and service to mankind, not just to Christians. That means if I see people who are not in the church, they're mankind, they're human—if I want to accept them, and I want to walk with them to influence their lives, then that is what I need to do in order to impact them. There are some races and cultures that if you don't go and live amongst them and come into their culture, you don't even have a place of favor to influence them to come into your world. I think we have failed miserably.

Ministry for us is not about black, white, straight, gay, Democrat, Republican, Pentecostal, Christian, non-Christian. That's not what ministry is to us. We have our beliefs. We have our fundamentals. We believe in demons. We believe in demonization. For us, ministry is about the human condition. There's no way that you're going to influence the millions of people that could come to the Lord if you don't develop a scope, a grip, a view of what is going on in the human condition. I know that's hard, because most of us can't see past our blocks, our fellowships, and our denominations. It is unfortunate that we're missing hearing creation groaning (Rom. 8), because we don't hear it. We have not tapped into the human condition, and right now people need to feel accepted.

Some of you have this hunger; you want to do this. You want to be an accepting minister, but you're afraid of the judgment of the people. You don't want to be like me. You don't want them to put you on a cross and have them make videos about you.

They do. We need to be careful about who we talk about and judge on social media. I'm not saying that judgment is not a part of Christianity, so don't take this the wrong way. Luke 6:37–38 says, "Judge not, and you will not be judged; condemn not, and you will not be condemned; forgive, and you will be forgiven; give, and it will be given to you. Good measure, pressed down, shaken together, running over, will be put into your lap. For with the measure you use it will be measured back to you." This is not a money scripture. It is a simple Golden Rule principle to live by.

I am heartbroken by some of the things that I see on Facebook and other social media. We have to realize—and care—that people have feelings; they have emotions. Some have children that can google and see the vicious, serpentile things some Christians say. We just go out and give our opinion, not understanding that not everybody agrees with what you do in your life. If everybody who didn't agree with every single thing you do got on social media and made you an outcast, talked about you negatively, you wouldn't like it. You have to give to people what you would desire to be given. I desire forgiveness. I desire mercy. So that's what I have to give.

But then a religious spirit blocks your understanding of your need for mercy. First of all, most religious people don't know they're religious. Second of all, religious people really, really,

really are principle driven. They are so determined to prove a point that they fail to reach people. That's why the more religious a church or a group becomes, the more narrow it gets, and it fails to receive people and minister to their needs.

We have to understand acceptance. This is how every destructive agenda in the world is outpacing the kingdom. The church wants to make people qualify for Calvary. They want to make people qualify for the anointing. They want to make sure that they look right enough and that they are beyond being questioned. Jesus said as Christians we would face all manner of evil (Matt. 5:11), but many of us are still trying to protect our reputation and image because we are really cosmetic, aesthetic, external Christians. There go your miracles. There goes your deliverance or the lack thereof. There goes your real authority. You have spent all your energy, you've become drained and exhausted with making sure you appear a certain way.

I think that if we really take time to get the brick out of our own eye, we won't be so occupied with judging people for every little thing that we don't agree with. When Paul wanted to be accepted and received in a place, he purposefully came very humble. He didn't come like he said the other apostles, the boastful ones, came. He came giving them his weakness, because he understood that we relate to each other not based upon our strengths, but based upon our weaknesses. If you will become more occupied with your weaknesses, then you will be accepted, and it will be easier for you to accept other people. I really think it's that self-righteousness that we have as a body, as a church, as believers, that makes us pompous. And then if we get knowledge—remember, the Bible talks about how knowledge puffs up, but it's love that edifies the church. If we don't prioritize love, regardless of what we know or what we don't know, and we don't stop pumping ourselves up thinking that we're better than everybody, then we could actually have a better aim.

I'm going to tell you what grieves me as a prophet—that puffing up. It is like how swelling in your body restricts the flow of something. This is why we are not supernatural people.

We have to rely on the flesh to persuade or condemn or judge or convince people. We don't have that problem at All Nations. The power of God moves in our midst very freely. Do you know why? Because we're not swollen up, or puffed up, using what we know to qualify. I want everybody. People tell us, "Well, you've got a bunch of people in All Nations with tattoos on their faces." But we also have church mothers. We have everybody. "Well, you've got all these gay men." Let me tell you something: every church in America has gay men and gay women, whether you know it or not. Where does the church want them to go? Should they not be there? The only difference is, at All Nations we actually have processes and context to minister to people who want to come out of a same-gender loving background or life, and we're not afraid of that. We're not intimidated by that.

My wife spent years ministering to people in the porn conventions. I can't go. I'm a seer. I don't want the images in my head, like some of the straight, suit-wearing preachers who are secretly porn addicts. I'm just telling you the truth. I could never go where my wife did and look at that, because that stuff would stay in me. You can wear a suit and do that. But there are people who are dying under the cancerous pressure, fighting, vying, competing to be accepted by church people, and we're just losing them. And we don't even care.

We say, "Hi, we're Christians. We have a conference." "Hi, we're Christians. Here's a book." "Hi, we're Christians. Here's a prayer shawl." And while we're doing that, recycling words and messages and strategies, hustling and branding, we're missing out on the harvest. I refuse to allow myself or anything my church does to be harvest negligent. We will preach holiness. We will preach deliverance. We will preach sin. But we're going to be harvest conscious.

We can't even get to deliverance and holiness if we don't accept people. We can't get them free if we don't accept them, if we don't become relatable. I don't care if you are white, black, a Buddhist, or a Muslim. We are all made in the image of God, and all have sinned and fallen short of the glory of God. We have some relatability right there, that I'm no better than you, you're no better than the next person—all of us. The determining factor is Jesus Christ, not you or not me. We have to start reprioritizing the way we think about this when it comes to unbelievers or people who are just not like us. The warning is this: if you don't, you're going to stay small, you're going to stay noninfluential, and you'll never have the ability to win your city. That's the warning. That's the cry of God: "I want to fill My house." The Great Commission can't be accomplished otherwise.

There is no reason why the church should not be overflowing with wandering, roaming souls. Revisit some of this stuff. I am not asking for you to agree. We don't have such low self-esteem that we're going to kill ourselves because you don't agree. But I love you. All Nations Church loves you. If you're Pentecostal, I love you. I'll dance with you. If you're Baptist, I love you. If you're Methodist, I love you. I love the PAWs. I love UPC. I love all of you, and I want you to know that my honest heart is the advancement of the kingdom. Do it the way God tells you to do it. Do it with your specific mission and assignment. But we are distracted. We're talking about jeans and color. We need to get this harvest.

Let's pull down the wall of hostility. Let's break down the division. Why? Because if we do it to the least of them, we've done it unto Him.

IN MY EXPERIENCE, some of the deliverance ministries, deliverance churches, and deliverance ministers I have encountered have been the most critical people on the planet. And as I have evolved into the real heart and essence and power of deliverance, what I've learned is that you cannot be a deliverer and be critical and faultfinding. Now, you can be direct, you can be abrasive, and you can even be sharp at times, but you cannot minister deliverance and be judgmental.

Jesus was most critical and judgmental of Pharisees and Sadducees. And the resemblance between those two regimes and what I see in the majority of our churches today is eerie—I mean, the resemblance is uncanny—especially considering two of the subjects we've been dealing with in this book: acceptance and appearance.

We should never say, "That young lady has a fast spirit." Have you ever heard that said about a woman just because she wears lip gloss or a tight skirt or leather? The same goes for "That young man has a spirit of perversion" or "That young lady has a spirit of rebellion." If you don't do deliverance, you don't qualify as a believable candidate to use those sentences.

You know, it's funny to hear people say that someone has a spirit of this or that when they don't cast out devils, and neither does their church. Now, they may stumble into a deliverance moment should a devil decide to speak up in a service—"Ha, we are many"—and then everybody says, "Oh, the blood, the blood, the blood." And they run the kids out and start chanting and all of that stuff because they don't know what else to do. But they are not actively engaging the powers of hell—and they couldn't be, because the minute they did, the devil would turn on them and claim the part of them that belongs to him because they are accusers. You cannot be an effective deliverance worker, deliverance minister, deliverance thinker, or a liberator if you are also an accuser.

I was thrown into deliverance ministry. That is my testimony. People always ask, "How did you say yes to deliverance ministry?" And I always tell people I did not said yes till I was tossed into deliverance ministry. Once I received the baptism of the Holy Ghost and the invisible world opened up to me, I immediately started running into the adversaries of God. And many of these adversaries that I saw and experienced were very comfortable in most churches, especially churches that were very harsh, judgmental, faultfinding, suspicious, and paranoid. We're going to untangle some of that in this chapter.

When you start dealing with deliverance, bondage, and

wickedness, the devil comes out of hiding. It is my belief that deliverance ministry is the most persecuted form of ministry. The devil does his best to make sure the truths of deliverance, the practice of deliverance, the culture of deliverance, and the word of deliverance stay obscure.

Deliverance ministry is very important. Jesus was a deliverance minister. I am going to discuss some basic principles about deliverance, including what it looks like, how it leads to holiness, and why it merits acceptance.

The Importance of Deliverance Ministry

First of all, deliverance was a promise given in the Old Testament—the deliverance of a people, deliverance through a Messiah. We know the on-again, off-again saga of Israel and its God, but we never really think about the third party in that threefold engagement: God's promises, God's words, God's way, God's judgments—and Israel's indecisiveness. The Book of Judges plainly says that Israel would turn to God and then disobey; they would turn to God, and then God would raise a deliverer. This cycle went on through the Book of Malachi and through the arrival of Jesus.

In the Old Testament we see every kind of power ministry. We see healing and the resurrection of the dead. We see provisional miracles, like when the prophet Elisha multiplied the widow's oil. (See 2 Kings 4:1–7.) We see geophysical miracles and judgments where seas and waters opened up (Exod. 14:15–31), and where rains opened up and fire came from heaven (1 Kings 18). One thing we did not see in the Old Testament was the casting out of devils. You never see in the Old Testament books a prophet, judge, or scribe dealing with and addressing a wicked or unclean spirit and casting it out. So, then, deliverance ministry and spiritual engagement is strictly a New Testament concept.

I believe you cannot be authentically New Testament and not be actively involved in deliverance ministry. You cannot say you're a New Testament, new covenant believer and not believe that deliverance is necessary, or not believe that deliverance is a priority.

After His resurrection, as a part of what many people call the Great Commission, Jesus said, "Whoever believes and is baptized will be saved, but whoever does not believe will be condemned" (Mark 16:16). The next thing that came out of Jesus' mouth was, "And these signs will accompany those who believe: in my name they will cast out demons" (v. 17). I just explained to you that for generations, for centuries, nobody had seen a demon cast out. Nobody had ever seen an evil, wicked spirit come out of somebody. This shows how much of a priority deliverance is to Jesus.

After saying, "All power is given unto me in heaven and in earth" (Matt. 28:18, KJV), Jesus tells His disciples in Luke 10:19, "Behold, I have given you authority to tread on serpents and scorpions, and over all the power of the enemy, and nothing shall hurt you." Also, the first thing Jesus gave the apostles in Matthew chapter 10 was not a ring (no shame for any of you to have them).

It wasn't a robe; it wasn't jet-black hair and a tie. It wasn't a miter, or a scepter, or a stamp, or a seal, or something from the Vatican. The first thing Jesus gave the apostles was authority over unclean spirits (v. 1). This is more evidence of how important deliverance is to Jesus.

In Luke chapter 4 we see a response or reaction from the kingdom of hell that further confirmed the authority of Jesus. Soon after Jesus had begun His earthly ministry, as He preached in the city of Capernaum (in the same chapter of Luke in which He preached Isaiah 61:1, "The Spirit of the Lord GOD is upon me, because the LORD has anointed me"), a demon cried out from the synagogue, saying, "What have you to do with us, Jesus of Nazareth? Have you come to destroy us? I know who you are—the Holy One of God" (Luke 4:34). To the powers of hell, Jesus' preaching represented judgment.

Now for those of you trying to figure out what this has to do with the religious spirit and criticism, my point is this: Jesus ministered deliverance for the first time not in the fields of Africa, not on a mission trip, and not under a healing tent. It was inside of a synagogue in front of traditional Jews who knew the Mosaic Law, the Mosaic codes, the Pentateuch, the Torah, the mission of the prophets, the law, and so forth. And yet one of the people who was supposedly clean, who may have been wearing a suit and a robe, had the spirit of a demon and needed deliverance. The Bible actually phrases it "he came out of him." A spirit spoke out of somebody who was in the temple, and Jesus addressed it, ordered it to be muzzled, and as the Bible phrases it, "he came out of him" (v. 35).

Deliverance is a priority in the New Testament. Deliverance is a culture. It is an act, an action. All the synoptic Gospels detail deliverance. I will discuss how deliverance and grace go hand in hand. The devil is actively working to pervert the gospel of grace. I believe he is doing it in a myriad of ways, including through the perversion of deliverance.

What Is a Demon?

First of all, let me quickly walk you through this. People always ask, "Well, what is a demon?" The majority of people believe that demons are fallen angels. Some people believe they are some pre-Edenic species of people that came under the judgment of God because of the engagement between angels and humans, the Nephilim. There are a lot of different theories out there.

The truth is—I'm going to give you a very intelligent theological answer—we don't know. We have no biblical trace or proof of their origin or where they came from, but we do know demons are older than the human race, and therefore smarter. We know that they are real, because Jesus cast them out, and He told us to cast them out as well.

There is another idea that demons came from when fallen angels had sex with humans, resulting in children who were giants, called Nephilim, and they were judged. At the point in which they were judged those evil spirits came out of them, and that explains how there has been such a multiplication. That's just a theological thing.

There are many theories about demons, and a lot of deliverance ministers have different ideas about the subject. But what we do know is that not all demons operate in the same way. The Bible talks about strongholds. I believe that demons operate in certain waters. I won't go into much detail about that here, but I will say we have Scripture to back it up. The first time in the Scriptures that the word *demon* is mentioned is in the Book of Deuteronomy:

> They sacrificed to demons that were no gods, to gods they had never known, to new gods that had come recently, whom your fathers had never dreaded.
>
> —Deuteronomy 32:17

This scripture shows that the Old Testament writers were aware of the existence of a species and a populace of celestial beings that were wholly evil, wholly wicked. These beings wanted leadership, influence, loyalty, and control. They wanted fidelity, but most importantly they wanted to compete. They wanted to persuade people—not just the people of God, but the whole human race—away from the purposes of God. It is the work of devils to torment, to seduce, to ensnare, to infiltrate, and to bring people away from the purposes of God. And they do this in a myriad of ways. They do it through sexuality and through perversion. They also do it through poverty—which, ironically, is one of the signs of the religious spirit.

Demons have been active since the Old Testament, but Jesus' arrival on the earth and His victory against the powers of hell (Col. 2:15) gave us the right to be those that *ekballō,* which means to throw out, to toss out, to unseat forcefully, or to remove or cast out a demon.[1] The first time this idea of race pops up is in Deuteronomy 32:17, which says, "They [Israel] sacrificed to false gods, which are not God" (NIV). So there are spiritual powers that want to play God.

"They sacrificed to false gods, which are not God—gods they had not known, gods that recently appeared" (NIV). Look at the way the Bible writer says this: "gods that recently appeared." I believe this means that in every generation, especially during Old Testament times, there was a different release and a thickly infiltrated environment of demonic spirits. One of the things that demons do is make sure you don't recognize them. I'm not going to say how—I'm going to leave that up to your imagination—but many demons are camouflaged. I don't think all demons always look demonic. This is why the gift of discerning of spirits is an addendum to the New Testament hardware of the believer.

Look at the phrase in verse 17, "gods that recently appeared, gods your ancestors did not fear" (NIV). Now, that is important because the word *gods* here is the word *sed* or *shed*, and it means "demon." It literally translates as "devil" or "devils."[2] Israel sacrificed to devils that were not God. They sacrificed to demons they did not know. So this means that in the on-again, off-again, whorish, adulterous relationship between Israel and its God, the whole problem was demons.

Now, if you've heard me preach, if you've heard me teach, if you follow my ministry, you know that I have a very simple philosophy about what is wrong with the world. It's so profound that it's one word: demons. Demons are what is wrong with the church. Demons are what is wrong with DC. Demons are what is wrong with the ozone layer. Demons are what is wrong in Afghanistan. Demons are what is wrong in Chicago. It's demons. Now, you may be reading this thinking, "Everything isn't about a demon." And not everything is. But a large portion of our problems are caused by demons, and Jesus demonstrates that by how often and how many of them He cast out.

The same Hebrew word *sed* or *shed*, translated "demons," is used again in Psalm 106:37: "They sacrificed their sons and their daughters to demons ["false gods" in the NIV]." Demons devour generations. They are human eaters, story eaters, future eaters, destiny eaters, calling eaters, and potential eaters. This means that if you are a Christian who uses your words to bite and devour, there is probably a spirit at work, an inside man reflected by your life and your words. The thing you host is what is driving you to act that way—it's a demon.

The Israelites sacrificed. They gave their children and their daughters over to false gods, to demons. That's what demons do.

They tear down and devour the future. They want to consume generations. Many churches are splitting because of demons. Many families are splitting because of demons.

There are many people who are preaching doctrine that is demonic. Just because you repeat something over and over again and chant it with your eyes in the back of your head, this does not make it real, right, or true. You may not believe that doctrine can be demonic, but Paul warned against "doctrines of devils" (1 Tim. 4:1, kjv). So just because somebody can substantiate, justify, highlight, or emphasize something by stringing a couple of scriptures together, that does not mean it is not demonic.

I believe it was a spirit of hatred and murder that caused people to use Bible scriptures to endorse slavery in early America, and to use Bible verses to continue to enslave African American people and justify their obedience to white slave owners. It was a spirit. Demons run the KKK. Demons run a lot of these hate organizations that mandate the murder, the consumption of the human race.

If you do a study of demons in the New Testament, you will find that when a person's appearance was recognized as demonic, often it was because the person wanted to be naked. They would tear their clothes and rip them off. So increased nakedness in a generation can also be demonic. Also, in self-hatred the demon-possessed person would throw himself into the fire with seizing.

I believe it was strong spirits or demons that would speak out through the Pharisees and Sadducees. They were demons of religion. Throughout the Word of God we find principles of deliverance from wickedness, deliverance from oppression, and deliverance from oppressors. Here is where our controversy is born. Many of us think that all oppression has to look oppressive, but there isn't such a thing as religious oppression. There are a lot of ways to enslave people. This is why I have the blood and the pulse of a deliverer running through my veins. Let me give you an idea.

If you go to a deliverance house or a deliverance church—if your vision is deliverance—what should you see when you walk into the church? Take a moment to ruminate, to ponder, to think. Should everybody sitting in the pews of a deliverance house be delivered? If that is true, then you are giving a redundant message to people that have already applied it. What should you say? Should you see people in all white? Should you see people that are already mature in their walk with God? Or should you see people that are in the middle of a war, a conflict? Should you see people that are battling philosophy? Should you see cross-dressers? Should you see drunks? Should you see liars? And should you see them in their raw form? My answer is an emphatic yes! I believe that when you go to a deliverance house, you should see everything in there. I think something is wrong with you and your church if I walk in and everybody looks whole. I automatically know there is a spirit of deception and dishonesty at work.

Somebody in one of those robes may be bound by porn.

Somebody in one of those pews may be cheating on his wife. Maybe one of the preachers on the roster has a spirit of depression caused by a demon, a spirit of heaviness. Somebody has got something. When we make room to create a tapestry of honesty where you see where people are, then we create room for the deliverance agenda to sweep through the house. And I'm going to tell you a secret: my church-growth strategy is not using beautiful cameras or watching and mimicking somebody else's story. From day one—before I could afford a camera or wonderful graphics, back when I was wearing big, wide-leg suits—my church-growth strategy was to cast the devil out. Many of our churches are dying because they won't do that.

For many people, what they think is demonic is actually just difference. We act as if anything aside from what we are used to is demonic, so we say it's a spirit of this or it's a spirit of that. But I believe you lose your right to use that phrase if you do not cast out devils.

CHAPTER 8

The Necessary Place

OBADIAH SETS THE stage for our discussion in this chapter. I am going to give you a tapestry and hope that as you continue to read about aesthetic, or cosmetic, Christianity, a hatred of hell will be born in you. I desire that you experience the zeal of the Lord Jehovah and that the same zeal that Jesus Christ had for His house consumes you. The by-product of this zeal will be a ministry of deliverance able to conquer warfare, bring deliverance, and break cults, occult practices, spells, and wizardry.

HOLINESS COMES AFTER

Obadiah 17 begins, "But upon Mount Zion." In this context I believe Mount Zion represents the church. Now, some may argue or believe it's something else, but for this discussion Zion is the high place of God. Zion is one of the things that God has called the church to be.

Obadiah 17 continues, "But upon Mount Zion there shall be deliverance" (KJV). It was promised to us. And after there is deliverance, "there shall be holiness" (KJV). Holiness does not precede deliverance. People don't come in the door holy, and they don't join your church holy. Deliverance must precede holiness.

Holiness is the way to real power, which is why many of us don't have it. We have not perfected holiness, and we cannot obtain power without it. Power is the fruit of a holy life. If the extent of the power that you see is happening during the laying on of hands or hitting someone's head and they fall down, that's not a sign of power. Gravity can achieve that alone. If the earth tilts one inch, the planet can accomplish someone falling. I am not impressed just because people are falling down. The real fruit of holiness is the power of God. There are a lot of impotent Christians who scream about holiness but have no fruit.

If your holiness cannot be examined by demonstration, then you have a form of godliness. A form does not produce power; you deny the power.

> Having the appearance of godliness, but denying its power. Avoid such people.
>
> —2 Timothy 3:5

An Inheritance

In the New International Version, Obadiah 17 reads: "But on Mount Zion will be deliverance; it will be holy, and Jacob will possess his inheritance."

Here we discover a threefold process: there will be deliverance;

then there will be holiness; and then there will be a release of possessions, promises, manifestations, destinies, and the future. Hebrews 11:3 clearly states that by God's word the worlds were framed. By His command was the invisible formed and made visible. Whatever God wants out of your life, it is unlocked through deliverance. I believe that people who are delivered are favored.

As people experience deliverance, they become preferred. I believe certain things open up because the less bound you are, the more trusted you are in heaven. God can release more to you with a life submitted to deliverance. It is imperative that you submit your life to the journey of deliverance. You cannot be a judgmental, harsh, or critical person and also be a deliverer.

Let's look at verse 21 of the same chapter:

> Deliverers will go up on Mount Zion to govern the mountains of Esau. And the kingdom will be the LORD's.
>
> —OBADIAH 1:21, NIV

The first phrase states, "Deliverers will go up on Mount Zion." That's exactly what we need right now in the body of Christ. We have a lot of preachers, a lot of singers—we have a lot of everything. You know what we don't have a lot of? Deliverers. People are too afraid to be touched to be deliverers. They are too afraid to be engaged with the human condition to be deliverers. They are too high, too exalted, too lofty. We are too busy measuring people up to be deliverers.

"Deliverers will go up on Mount Zion to govern the mountains of Esau" (NIV). That means when a person is a deliverer, she rules in the midst of her adversaries. She governs in the face of her opponents. "To govern the mountains of Esau. And the kingdom will be the LORD's." This correlates with Jesus' New Testament statement in Matthew 12:28: "If I cast out devils by the Spirit of God, then the kingdom of God is come unto you" (KJV).

We are a kingdom church, and we are kingdom believers. We have a kingdom company, a kingdom idea. A kingdom is not religion.

Where Is Your Deliverance?

Where is your deliverance? When was the last time you cast a devil out? Do you believe in spiritual engagement? Do you know the names of demons? Do you understand how many of them operate?

Emancipation, freedom, and liberty are found in the kingdom. If it is not operating with the goal of freeing people, it is not the kingdom. The kingdom is all about righteousness, joy, and peace in the Holy Ghost.

> For the kingdom of God is not a matter of eating and drinking but of righteousness and peace and joy in the Holy Spirit.
>
> —Romans 14:17

The kingdom does not come by observation. It's not about how many buildings you have, how many record labels you possess, or how many companies you start. All of that can be entrepreneurial and not be of the kingdom. Often we use the words *entrepreneurial* and *kingdom* synonymously. We can imitate something, and it can be innovative, but it doesn't make you or the product kingdom driven, especially if what's driving you is not the Spirit of Jesus Christ the deliverer.

Accepting the Outcast

The Book of Joel explains why we accept the outcast:

> And it shall come to pass, that whosoever shall call on the name of the Lord shall be delivered: for in mount Zion and in Jerusalem shall be deliverance, as the Lord hath said, and in the remnant whom the Lord shall call.
>
> —Joel 2:32, kjv

This is why we want the drug addict. This is why we want the people with piercings in their eyebrows. This is why we want the people with dreadlocks. We want people who live with and without precepts, the victims and the victimizers.

Do you know that the mother of the very first murderer was also the mother of the first person murdered? The very first act of wickedness on the planet after man disobeyed God was a murder, and the same mother birthed both the victim and the victimizer (Gen. 4:1–16).

If you are not a deliverance minister, your instinct is probably to take the side of the victim and leave the victimizer to be ensnared. People become victimizers because they have not been freed by the ministry of deliverance. There is no such thing as outgrowing a devil. You can mature and outgrow some things, but you cannot get smart enough to intellectually outwit a demon. What I love about deliverance ministry, and therefore grace, is that we are effective with victims, and we are effective with victimizers.

Dressed to Suppress

The appearance and aesthetics of the church have suppressed many of us. Appearance and aesthetics will coach you: "Keep that in. Put on your collar. Keep that in. Put on your suit. Don't let people see that. Absolutely not." When things begin to surface, and you allow yourself to be freed by the power of deliverance, then maturity comes, and after that advancement and Godlikeness, which is the evidence of holiness exemplified in your life, not in your makeup or appearance. I love Joel 2:32, and I am challenging every pastor, every preacher, every business owner, every life coach, every strategic warfare prayer specialist, every women's day leader, the dating expert—all of you. I'm challenging you all to become deliverance ministers.

Our churches will always be filled with thousands of people because of Joel 2:32 and the "whosoever" factor. It is not gender specific or based on sexual preference, or what a person is wearing, or who a person is dating—it says "whosever." Whosoever, regardless of what they are wearing; whosoever, whatever they've done; whosoever, whatever they are involved in; whosoever, whatever areas in which they're going to fall. There are people who don't like or agree with the Word of God but that makes no difference to who can call; it just makes it available to those who are willing to call.

The Bible states "whosoever," which translates to "whatsoever." If you become a whosoever and whatsoever kind of preacher, then authority will flow. It would shock you to experience the level of authority released in a whosoever leader and believer. When you have this kind of authority, there is no need to announce it to the devil; he already knows who you are. Demons will recognize you because they are afraid of the authority a whosoever and whatsoever believer carries. As a matter of fact, demons hate the type of authority mentioned in Joel 2:32: "And whosoever calls upon the name of the LORD shall be saved…" But there is a semicolon.

Dwelling Place

Joel 2:32 continues, "For in Mount Zion," which is the dwelling place of God, "and in Jerusalem shall be deliverance" (KJV). The process, the act, and the decision of God is to set His people free from their oppressors. The New International Version continues, "There will be deliverance, as the Lord has said, even among the survivors whom the Lord calls." You can be saved and not delivered.

I believe there is a demon with a seat in every world religion. The Old Testament idols, things people bow to; the golden calf, Baal, Ashtoreth, and the goddess Diana—do you think those were only statues? Who do you think demanded them? Demons. Demons outsmarted the human race by creating a religious ideology that caused people to worship things and not God. Religion wins people's fidelity. I believe demons conspired to win people by starting a religion. And people followed the images and idol vessels. It worked.

Many of these campaigns against the Son of God actually use the name Jesus while perpetrating demonic agendas. I believe these were devised by the collaboration of demons. Paul called this "another Jesus":

> For if someone comes and proclaims another Jesus than the one we proclaimed, or if you receive a different spirit from the one you received, or if you

> accept a different gospel from the one you accepted, you put up with it readily enough.
>
> —2 Corinthians 11:4

There is not just another Jesus floating around there, but we can infer from this scripture that there are many false Christs. "We" acknowledge "another Jesus" that people claim, but this "Jesus" does not rebuke people and tell people when they are wrong. He doesn't correct or challenge them. He holds hands with Buddha and Krishna and does yoga from time to time. People have proclaimed a Jesus with no right or wrong and who doesn't care what you do or have any merit regarding life decisions. No, that is not the Jesus of the Bible. That is culturally-modified-with-the-cultural-preservatives Jesus. It is the jam Jesus.

Many people come up with a concept of God that we can live with, one who will agree with us. But when you go into deliverance ministry, you learn that there is just and unjust, righteous and wicked, holy and unholy.

Ministry of Love

Deliverance ministry looks through the eyes of grace. It works and processes people through God's love. And it establishes a life of holiness and the unadulterated fruit of life through Christ Jesus.

Maybe you are reading this and you are a lesbian, a crackhead, a porn addict, or a weed head; it doesn't matter if your father molested you, if you've had twenty abortions, if you are a sex addict, or if you are on the down low; if you are asexual, homosexual, bisexual, or transsexual—one of the greatest lies that hell is perpetuating right now is that deliverance is not available to you. But deliverance is available to all of you. You cannot do this in your own strength. Find a house of God that hates hell, a church that is going to love on you until they love the hell out of you.

That house will grab your head and minister to you without fear of who you are, what you did, what you have, or where you came from. They will love you enough to bind the devil, minister deliverance, and help you work that deliverance out. Let church people argue about what you look like and what's going on with you—you need to find a safe place, a house of God that preaches and ministers deliverance. Amen.

CHAPTER 9

The Journey

I WANT TO JOURNEY through some things as I continue to discuss deliverance, maintaining deliverance, and entering holiness. I can't really talk about the topic of deliverance without talking about grace, because deliverance comes from grace. Some people confuse grace and mercy. Mercy is withholding the punishment that you deserve, but grace empowers you not to be in bondage to sin.

As you enter and maintain deliverance and holiness, one of the first decisions you must make is whether you will allow the grace of God to usher you through the process or allow your works to usher you there. You cannot have it both ways. Romans 11:6 says, "But if it is by grace, it is no longer on the basis of works; otherwise grace would no longer be grace." You will either put your faith toward the grace of God or your own goodness.

As we journey through the Scriptures, I am going to show you that when you put your faith in the grace of God to help you walk through deliverance, you will succeed! Some parts of this journey, especially our discussion of Romans chapter 6, may shock you. The journey will first provide you with understanding, and then it will reestablish your identity. It is hard to believe that you can be delivered until you first understand who you are and your identity in Christ. That is what I am going to help you walk through, so that you will be encouraged.

If you are going to be a deliverance minister, you must get delivered yourself. Some of you may be wondering, "Do preachers require deliverance? What if they have a large social media following?" The answer is yes! Everyone, regardless of their title or status, needs to work out the process of deliverance. I am now going to talk about what that process looks like.

The Process of Grace

Ephesians 2:1–2 talks about how before Christ, we were dead in our transgressions and we followed the ways of the law. Let me say, sin has already been judged! This means if you are saved and have received Jesus Christ as your Lord and Savior, your sin has been judged. However, your sin still has consequences, which is one reason why you need the grace of God to be able to conquer some of those things.

> What shall we say then? Shall we continue in sin, that grace may abound?
>
> —Romans 6:1, kjv

Paul talks about the gospel, which is the good news, the grace. Because he preached grace so well, people questioned, "If it's all about what Jesus Christ did on the cross, does that mean our works mean nothing? Can we continue living in the flesh?" These are valid questions you too may be faced with if you have proficiently taught the meaning of grace.

Paul dissected. God had given him a dispensation, a revelation, and he taught it very thoroughly. Due to Paul's thoroughness, the question arose, "Can we sin, if grace is going to abound?" Of course, the answer is no. Grace is not something that helps you do what you want to do. As a matter of fact, the grace of God and the message of grace will cause people to open what is already there. Grace will not make you start doing something that you were not doing or that was not in your heart to do. It essentially exposes people in their sin. Can we keep on sinning? Paul says in Romans 6:2, God forbid! Absolutely not!

> How shall we, that are dead to sin, live any longer therein? Know ye not, that so many of us as were baptized into Jesus Christ were baptized into his death? Therefore we are buried with him by baptism into death: that like as Christ was raised up from the dead by the glory of the Father, even so we also should walk in newness of life.
>
> —Romans 6:2–4, KJV

> Knowing this, that our old man is crucified with him, that the body of sin might be destroyed, that henceforth we should not serve sin.
>
> —ROMANS 6:6, KJV

Now that's an interesting statement. "The body of sin" means that sin had a body that was within us that has been crucified. It had a host, and that body had to experience the same death that Jesus did. "That the body of sin might be destroyed" means it has been done away with—it's dead, it's destroyed. For example, if you are eating a cheeseburger and you think to yourself, "What happened to that cheeseburger? I destroyed that cheeseburger," you know the cheeseburger is not coming back. It's done, it's gone. The same is true with sin: the body of sin was "destroyed, that henceforth we should not serve sin."

Therefore, holiness is important, and the reason why we should choose holiness is because the body of sin is done. Your old nature is dead. You don't have to keep resurrecting it and killing it. Some individuals use Paul's statement in 1 Corinthians 15:31, "I die daily," to mean that the old, sinful nature comes up and we need to continually kill it. In context Paul was saying, "The resurrection has not come, so why are we going through all of this? Why am I dying daily? Why am I going through all this persecution?" He was not referring to killing his old nature daily; he was stating that his old nature had been completely destroyed.

I want to point out a few things as we continue to journey through the old nature. Some of you may have questions about the old nature being completely done. Your old nature is dead once you are in Christ. That's encouraging, right? Some people may ask, "If the old nature is completely dead, why do I struggle? Why do I continue to sin? Why can't I get my deliverance?" The answer to those questions is simple: your mind must be renewed. Your mind is like a programmed system. When you were in that old nature, you had habits and lust issues. You were selfish and had unclean possessions. When you have habits, they become natural to you—that is the old nature. It left an imprint on your programming system, which is your brain. Now you have to be reprogrammed by renewing your mind with the Word of God.

> And be not conformed to this world: but be ye transformed by the renewing of your mind, that ye may prove what is that good, and acceptable, and perfect, will of God.
>
> —Romans 12:2, KJV

When you struggle, it may not necessarily be caused by your sin; you struggle because your mind must be renewed. Sin does not cause the sin nature, because as a Christian you don't have a sin nature. That nature has been killed. What you have is a problem with your mind being unrenewed. Newness of the mind allows Christians to experience the righteousness of God in Christ. Righteousness is available, but you must know and believe it. If you do not believe, then your deliverance will not happen. You must believe in your deliverance; that your identity is in Christ and that you are the righteousness of Christ. As Romans 6:7 states, "For he that is dead is freed from sin" (KJV). You must choose freedom. Not all individuals choose this freedom, even when it's available to them.

Having an unrenewed mind does not mean that righteousness is not available. It does not mean that freedom in unavailable. It simply means that your mind needs to be renewed. If you have a new nature, if you are the righteousness of God, then you don't have to let sin rule over your life. You have been given freedom.

> Now if we be dead with Christ, we believe that we shall also live with him: knowing that Christ being raised from the dead dieth no more; death hath no more dominion over him. For in that he died, he died unto sin once: but in that he liveth, he liveth unto God.
>
> —ROMANS 6:8–10, KJV

That old man has died, so why would you choose to operate in sin if the old nature has been put to death?

> Neither yield ye your members as instruments of unrighteousness unto sin: but yield yourselves unto God, as those that are alive from the dead, and your members as instruments of righteousness unto God.

> For sin shall not have dominion over you: for ye are not under the law, but under grace.
>
> —Romans 6:13–14, kjv

The grace of God has the power to put sin to death. It is extremely important that you understand that you are the righteousness of Christ. If you lack this understanding, it may make you feel that you have to prove yourself, but you don't because Scripture says you are righteous. Where there is law, there is knowledge of sin. When you go into those legalistic patterns, you keep yourself bound and are incapable of operating in the grace of God the way you need to. It is the grace of God that puts all of that to death.

You are under grace!

> For sin shall not have dominion over you: for ye are not under the law, but under grace. What then? Shall we sin, because we are not under the law, but under grace? God forbid. Know ye not, that to whom ye yield yourselves servants to obey, his servants ye are to whom ye obey; whether of sin unto death, or of obedience unto righteousness?
>
> —Romans 6:14–16, kjv

The Door of Holiness

What you yield to, you give room to and open the door to. If you yield to sin, then you open the door to sin. This is why choosing to walk in holiness is important. Yielding to sin opens the door to Satan. There are reasons why you should choose to be holy. It has nothing to do with God's love for you or trying to prove how accepted you are; but if you open the door to Satan, he will try to devour you. He has a purpose; he has an aim. Living holy will protect you and your relationships, soften your heart, and allow you to know what it means to grow in the Lord. You do not want to open yourself to death, depression, anxiety, poverty, and other ungodly things that are by-products created when you yield to Satan.

> But God be thanked, that ye were the servants of sin, but ye have obeyed from the heart that form of doctrine which was delivered you. Being then made free from sin, ye became the servants of righteousness. I speak after the manner of men because of the infirmity of your flesh: for as ye have yielded your members servants to uncleanness and to iniquity unto iniquity; even so now yield your members servants to righteousness unto holiness. For when ye were the servants of sin, ye were free from righteousness.
>
> —Romans 6:17–20, kjv

Verse 19 says, "I speak after the manner of men because of the infirmity of your flesh" (kjv). In other words Paul is saying you're not spiritually mature enough to understand this, so I came down to your level to help you to understand this principle.

Verse 20 goes on to state, "For when ye were the servants of sin, ye were free from righteousness" (KJV). In other words, you cannot be righteous based on your own goodness. This does not mean that people who are not saved cannot do good things, because they can and will. However, they are still bound people.

The hold of righteousness cannot reach you in your own good works. But guess what? The opposite is also true. You are now freed from sin because of the righteousness of God. If you commit sin, the hold of sin still cannot have you. I know it sounds too good to be true, but sin does not open up the door for your old nature to return. You have the righteousness of Christ. However, you can opt out of righteousness by choosing not to serve God. You may also opt out by deciding to yield to the things of the enemy. Just as righteousness could not have you from your good works, neither can sin from your bad works.

Paul is making a point to allow you to understand how solidified you are in the righteousness of Christ. I am not talking about an issue of heaven or hell. I'm establishing that when you receive Christ, you receive the righteousness of Christ, and nothing you do can cause sin to take hold of you—there's nothing that can stop you from living holy. That's the bottom line, and that is immensely encouraging. There is no hold that can stop you from living holy!

> What fruit had ye then in those things whereof ye are now ashamed? For the end of those things is death. But now being made free from sin, and become

> servants to God, ye have your fruit unto holiness, and the end everlasting life.
>
> —Romans 6:21–22, kjv

What fruit could you possibly possess in the old nature if it leads to death? Holiness is a fruit, not a root. What does that mean? You cannot strive to be holy and make that your foundation in Christ. Holiness comes after the foundation has been laid by grace, through faith. This makes holiness a fruit and not a root, because it is a response to a life of faith in God. If you make holiness the root, you are going to run out of grace, which can lead you to the road of backsliding. When you are in your flesh, you cannot please God.

> For the wages of sin is death; but the gift of God is eternal life through Jesus Christ our Lord.
>
> —Romans 6:23, kjv

> And this is eternal life, that they know you, the only true God, and Jesus Christ whom you have sent.
>
> —John 17:3

Eternal life and everlasting life are different. *Eternal* means to exist forever; without end or beginning. *Everlasting* means to last a long time. The wages of sin is death, but the gift of God is to know Him. The gift is for Him to be revealed to you. That gift cannot happen outside of the grace of God. If you don't know or believe in Christ, there's no way for you to maintain your deliverance, and no way for you to live holy. But the gift that God has given us is eternal life, to know Him, and to be empowered so that we can live lives of righteousness and holiness. However, we cannot do that if we don't see ourselves correctly in the Scriptures.

The Spirit and the Soul

Some people may ask, "What part of an individual needs deliverance? Is it the spirit?" I think it is important to know where demons go, because if holiness is the fruit and not the root, that means demons are not effective in the spirit. Demons have to occupy themselves in root systems, root issues, or anything that is rooted under the ground. It is never an obvious issue or easily seen.

Even though we are the righteousness of Christ, we still must deal with carnality. This is because though we are spirits, we are also living souls. When we are born again, our spirit becomes one with Christ. The old man or nature dies, and His Spirit and our spirit become one. The spirit is where the incorruptible seed is planted. Although we are one with God in the spirit, we must experience Him in our souls. Jesus gave His soul so He could reap souls, not spirits. The spirit is already made perfect in the Lord.

As we process life, we process it through our souls. In order to receive deliverance, the spirit part of man must affect the soul part of man. Ephesians 3:17 talks about the inner man being rooted and grounded in the Spirit. This means the Spirit of God has to have influence on your soul. If God speaks to me by the Spirit right now and says, "Snap your fingers," and I do decide to snap my fingers, was it my spirit or my soul that obeyed God? Your soul must obey God. That is where deliverance happens. Demonic spirits operate in the soulish part of man, and so it's the soulish part of man that requires deliverance. Some people have all of God in their spirit and none of God in their soul; this is how carnal Christians are formed.

An individual can possess the spirit of God but not be influenced in his or her habits, decisions, or thought life. There is no renewing of the mind; thus again, you can be the righteousness of Christ but not manifest the righteousness of Christ.

To be demonized means that demons are in your soul. These demons are not just hanging out or making you do bad things. They are mentoring you, disciplining you, and conforming your thoughts and your belief systems. They conform you, so when they are cast out, guess who's left? You! How do you cast yourself out?

Demonization goes beyond the soul. When a demon is cast out, if your mental capacity has been formed and shaped, then you still have an issue to deal with. Being delivered does not mean that you are automatically going to live holy. Job was demonized, the Bible says, because of his mentality, his belief. He was operating in fear, anxiety, and doubt. While at the height of his demonization, the thing that Job said the most, many Christians say as a testimony: "Though he slay me, yet will I trust in him" (Job 13:15, KJV). God didn't kill Job. Job's soul expressed that while under demonization and oppression in his soul. He did not have a sober mind at the time. In Job 3:25 he stated, "For the thing that I fear comes upon me, and what I dread befalls me." It was a manifestation of something that he feared. He feared losing his possessions.

Demonization can go beyond demons being in the soul. My definition of demonization is when you harmonize your beliefs, thoughts, and opinions with a life against God's will. This belief system opposes God's Word and His promises and is considered the belief and doctrines of devils.

Your belief system has everything to do with your decisions and your paradigm of life, which is the place of the soul, the mind, the will, and the emotions. In 2 Corinthians 10:9 Paul states, "I do not want to appear to be frightening you with my letters," because the first place of warfare is in our views and our opinions, as it says in 2 Corinthians 10:5, "casting down imaginations, and every high thing that exalteth itself against the knowledge of God, and bringing into captivity every thought to the obedience of Christ" (KJV). The first place where we must fight spiritual warfare and the demonic is our mind.

After the Deliverance

You may require counseling after the deliverance process. Do not think that just because you went through the deliverance process and demons were cast out of you, you are no longer demonized. Your mind may still be demonized, and you can't cast that out. Your mind can only be renewed. Again, the first place of warfare is the mind. Any mentality or thought that goes against the knowledge of God, any thought that combats the truth, is a thought that needs to be renewed and is an issue of deliverance.

Because I am discussing spiritual warfare, I must discuss Ephesians 6. I will not go through all of it, just a couple of scriptures. I will begin with verse 13: "Therefore take up the whole armor of God, that you may be able to withstand in the evil day, and having done all, to stand firm."

Ephesians 6:17 says, "And take up the helmet of salvation, and the sword of the Spirit, which is the word of God." Many times we use the sword of the Spirit to try to fight Satan instead of using it for ourselves. If you are going to be delivered, you need to know something about the Word of God in order to war with the sword of the Spirit—not against the enemy, but for yourself.

Consider how when temptation came to Jesus in the Book of Matthew, He was led into the wilderness by the Spirit (4:1). It is interesting that the Bible says when He came out of the wilderness, He was full of the power of the Spirit. Something had to have transpired while He was in the wilderness. Jesus was tested to be able to use the Word of God. One thing I find interesting in that passage of Scripture is that when the enemy came to tempt Jesus, Jesus pulled out the Word of God from His heart, from within Him. As Psalm 119:11 says, "I have stored up your word in my heart, that I might not sin against you." As Jesus spoke during the temptation, He used the Word of God. He did not use it against Satan—Satan had been listening to the Word of God since the beginning. Jesus used the Word of God for Himself. And what did He say? "Man shall not live by bread alone" (Matt. 4:4). Who is man? Himself, not Satan. We must submit ourselves to the Word of God, especially with regard to deliverance.

Matthew 4 verses 7 and 10 say, "You shall not put the Lord your God to the test....You shall worship the Lord your God and him only shall you serve." Jesus demonstrated that He used Scripture He had hidden to make sure He would respond in holiness and righteousness when temptation came. Be sure to understand that when I'm talking about spiritual warfare, and when I'm talking about putting on the armor of God and the helmet of salvation, our own armor is the Word, and we are using it to make sure that we stay free. The Bible says in Hebrews 4:12, "The word of God is living and active, sharper than any two-edged sword, piercing to the division of soul and of spirit." You must obey and submit to the Word of God. When it comes to freedom and deliverance, you must submit yourself, your mindset, your will, your decisions, and your habits. You must subject all these things to the Word of God because that is where you will find protection and freedom.

A PERSUASIVE ENCOUNTER

Deliverance is a fruit or by-product of grace. The Bible says that Jesus was full of grace and truth, and with this grace and truth He ministered deliverance to people. Why? It is the work of the soul that allows room for the life in the Spirit to be born. Many people are under stress and strain trying to live life in and by the Spirit without having done the work in the soul. Sadly, people do not work out the issues of the soul because they don't know how. The church, unfortunately, does not aid in the renewing of the soul, and it is impossible to engage the soul of a man without encountering whatever is occupying it.

Many people allow these things to go on because they don't believe that a Spirit-filled, blood-bought believer can be possessed. That is a horrible translation from King Jimmy; but the real word I've been employing is *demonization*. There can be areas of a believer's personality and choices he or she makes that are influenced by external entities that are not the Spirit of God. Demons are spirits that work in the soul, that talk in the soul.

Some of you were jarred when I suggested earlier that demons coach, minister, and encourage. But here is why: if they are spirit beings (and we know that they are, because they're people without bodies), they have real personalities, real motives, real agendas, and real things they want to do. This is why their ultimate punishment and their ultimate fear is to be cast out. That's how we war against them—by commanding them to come out of a body. Demons do most of their work in the physical realm, but to do so they need a physical partner. They need a decision from the person's soul that allows them to do their work.

There is a saying, "Sin lies at the door." The Bible says not to give place to the devil, a foothold to Satan. Where there is a door, there is a room. If your body is a temple, then the Holy Ghost is not the only thing trying to occupy it. If the devil wants worship, one of the places he wants to be enthroned is in your life. It becomes his abode, his house. There are a lot of people that are bound, trying to strive toward freedom in the spirit and strive toward holiness, but they can't because they have not experienced deliverance.

Hyper-grace people want to act like demons and deliverance are not a real thing. Here is my major conflict with the hyper-gracers: Jesus did it, so that is proof that deliverance works. Hyper-grace believers believe there are no devils, and that they do not have to worry about the devil. All they need to do is meditate, do some crossword puzzles, roll their eyes, and put some incense on. They believe they are a new creature because Jesus did everything. Well, here is the problem, buddy. Paul was the recipient of the gospel of grace, which is why he confronted Peter. Paul himself was the recipient of grace, as he studied at the feet of Gamaliel.

When Paul was on the island of Arabia, God downloaded to

him what He wanted to do through the agenda of grace, and he cast out devils. Paul, who was a grace custodian, a grace author, a grace contributor to the document of the New Testament, literally cast devils out of witches and sorcerers. He cast devils out of people and cast out demons of infirmities. To be in on grace does not exempt you from your obligation to do the work and spiritually engage the powers of hell. Here is one thing you're going to realize when you're dealing with massive populations of people: It's impossible for you to be effective and not have a deliverance ministry. Where there are masses, there will be monsters.

Most people that criticize others who are free don't affect masses. They have a mini-thing, mini-churches, and mini-phone lines. They don't like people with messages that reach the masses. But the masses respond to ministers who preach freedom, who seem to have answers. When people learned that my ministry casts out devils, does deliverance ministry, and flows in the healing power of God, it did not stop them from coming. Visitors have not stopped coming. Why? Deliverance does its own work, and deliverance promotes itself. When you see freed lives, progressive lives, changed families, and changed children, people begin to come.

The Bible calls us slaves. We were slaves to sin (Rom. 6:20). If we were slaves to sin, then who is the perpetrator of the sin nature, the synergy of the sin consciousness? Satan! Who requires deliverance but a slave? If you are a slave, it means you are owned by a thing; and sin is a person and a personality. Deliverance is a miracle ministry because it prevents people from becoming slaves. Thus, acceptance is the catalyst to deliverance, and deliverance does not happen prior to acceptance. Acceptance must be at the door—not judgment nor criticism nor name-calling nor anything negative. The doorway is acceptance, love, and the value we see in others. Jesus died for you—now let's work on you! You cannot work on the one you haven't won.

Just because an individual has joined the church, it doesn't mean you have won that person. Even if she agrees with your doctrine, it does not mean you've won her. I don't believe you can win people in thirty seconds. I think there are people who have to be convinced and, like Paul said, "fully persuaded" (Rom. 4:21, KJV). A person can only be fully persuaded once they've overcome being partially persuaded. Being "fully" something means that something has graduated, grown, or matured. Many of you are condemning, judging, and talking about people that are not even fully persuaded. You can tell they're not persuaded by their meanderings, their roaming, their vacillations between heaven and hell, between the power of hell and the power of God. In Acts 26:18 Paul said his commission was to turn them "from the power of Satan to God."

Agents of Deliverance

In order to operate a deliverance ministry, we cannot be afraid of people's bondage. We can't be afraid to be associated with it, be around it, or engage it. You must be a liberated agent in order to do that. So here are some things you need to realize. In a healthy deliverance agenda in a deliverance church you're going to find these things. You're going to be talking about strongholds, principalities, bondages, and different ways or different operational facilities in a life that the devil operates in. When you're dealing with life in the Spirit, as Paul said, "Walk by the Spirit, and you will not gratify the desires of the flesh" (Gal. 5:16).

Here's how it works: Flesh cannot be cast out. The mind cannot be cast out. Dysfunction cannot be cast out. A personality cannot be cast out. There may be something demonic forming, grooming, or materializing. The Holy Spirit is a teacher. He teaches us. He leads us into truth. If demons as spirit beings do the opposite of what the Holy Spirit does, then the Holy Spirit leads you into truth or guides you. It's a spirit being; it has a spiritual agenda.

The problem is, we have several correlating issues that we are treating as the same thing: First you repent of sin; flesh, you crucify; your mind, you renew—but a demon, you cast out. We act like all of that can be handled in a one-stop shop, but it cannot. They are four different things that operate in four different ways.

Flesh, you must crucify. Tell it no. However, you can't tell the flesh no if the mind is not renewed and you are not relying on the Spirit of God. All these things are integrated. These streams, when they are active in a house, will draw a lot of prisoners, a lot of slaves. Christians are supposed to be the liberators, the emancipators, but we act like prison guards. We act as if it's our job to preach until people stay bound by condemning them and prophesying demonic faith on them through hate speech and hate language. We are supposed to emancipate people, to bring them out of whatever is holding them.

The Bible talks about how when an unclean spirit is gone out of a man, it goes in dry places seeking and not finding rest. How does a devil find rest? By being at home in a life. Then the demon says to itself, "I will go back to my home." A demon sees your life as its personal real estate. "I will go back to my home" shows a struggle; it shows a tug-of-war; and so it shows a commitment to a life, a commitment to a generation.

There are certain demons that are assigned to a family name. Just as you may say, "I'm in the Johnson family," "I'm in the Smith family," or "I'm in the McIntyre family," demons of death or demons of poverty can be assigned to a family. What happens is in a moment of truth, which is how hunger is activated, somebody deviates from the direction of a whole family story. This person learns that deliverance is available and there's a demonic spirit that the person must remove, or *ekballō*, from the soul.

There is only one thing that can remove a devil, and that is the Word of God. You can't physically remove a devil. Beating someone or banging somebody's head with a Bible is not going to remove a devil.

I believe in the laying on of hands because it is a transmission of the power of God. What makes the laying on of hands effective is the authority of the Word of God. That is why Jesus spoke to demons and cast them out. Jesus said in John 6:63, "The words that I have spoken to you are spirit," so if words are spiritual, then it takes a spiritual instrument to unseat a spiritual being. You must say, "Come out." You confront the spirit by identifying what it is, and you command it to come out. Command that demon to be evicted from its spiritual host so that the person's soul can then be repaired through discipleship and the truth of the Word of God.

I believe that one of the reasons why people don't receive the Holy Ghost is because of demonic occupancy. I believe there are demons who work to make sure that people don't receive the baptism of the Holy Ghost. Jesus used the term *ekballō*, which means to cast out or to throw out violently. Deliverance is a hostile ministry. It is a love ministry. It is a passionate ministry. It is a ministry of mercy. When people say *ekballō*, they say "Come out!" by the authority of the Word of God and the person's decision to unseat the spirit. Often when we're ministering deliverance to people, we say, "He doesn't want the spirit anymore. He renounces the demonic spirit and makes a decision to live his life under the Word of God." That gives us the legal right to unseat the devil.

When you are in agreement with something, when you are in partnership with the thing, and when your life is set up in such a way to accommodate the thing, then you have no basis and no grounds other than God's will by which to be delivered. God wants you delivered, but He will only deliver you from your adversaries; He will leave you with your friends. If you are friends with a thing or spirit, there is no motivation for you to be set free from it. It is very important that you recognize this. Your soul has to be repaired through counsel, relationship, needs, love, and affection, but most importantly through truth. Many people go back into bondage and leave the work of grace because they don't have enough truth.

Here is the harsh truth: if you are in a church where the preaching is less than quality, it will be difficult to receive your freedom. What you require is a high level of revelation and truth to continue to transform your soul to live under the leadership of the Holy Spirit. Some of you are bound not because you want to be but because your preachers are just not good enough. Their messages don't contain any substance. For example, if you are in a flesh war and fighting a very aggressive spirit of witchcraft, and you go to church every week to hear, "This is the last time you're going to cry about this," you are basically hearing a prison sentence. You do not need something that will produce strife in you but something that is going to awaken the ability that is within your spirit to teach you how to respond to that stronghold. Deliverance is vital, and it is critical that you engage it, because it makes you more reliant on the grace of God.

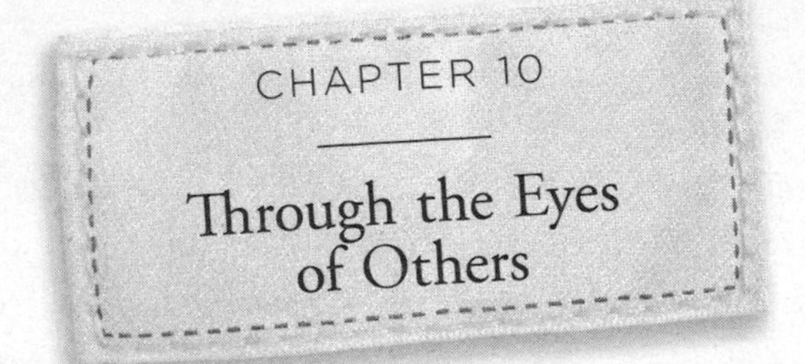

CHAPTER 10

Through the Eyes of Others

NEXT WE WILL deal with deliverance and appearance. Can deliverance affect your appearance? Maybe, maybe not. But bondage can affect your appearance. People think looking a certain way testifies a certain degree of freedom. I believe that looking a certain way can also testify a certain degree of bondage, particularly depending upon the lens that you're looking through. You can't always use appearance as the sign of the symptom of someone's liberation or freedom, when it is a spiritual issue dependent on many factors.

Many people believe in modesty. Some of you say "modest" but really mean dated, ugly, old, or beyond attraction. Modest doesn't have to mean ugly. Things can be attractive and modest. I believe to be modest means to be protective of and deliberate about not engaging and intentionally making people have sexual desire or intentions toward you. This is a fine line. You may say, "I'm distracted because of the clothing you are wearing. Your attire is not modest at all." If so, you are projecting your personal bondage onto that individual. This is not a clothing issue, it is a stronghold issue.

Matthew 18:9 says, "If your eye causes you to sin, tear it out and throw it away." Titus 1:15 says, "To the pure, all things are pure." It's simple—you need help controlling your eyeballs. You can't use your bondage to control somebody else's shopping habits. By the same token, people should not shop with the intention or the motivation to ensnare, allure, or captivate. You got your "go get them" dress on or your "go get them" shirt on, and you want your cleavage out to make sure that people are captivated and under your spell with the wrong intentions. However, I am a balanced person. I believe a person can be captivated by a tight shirt or by a robe. I believe both items send the same message. Just because a robe is not tight, that doesn't mean it isn't hypnotizing. If you think that everything in a robe is holy, then you've already been hypnotized.

There are many Catholic priests that wear robes, and the scent of the boys they've devoured and molested is still on them. Do not believe that appearance testifies one way or the other. I think it's a semantic issue, and as a people we need to stop going back and forth about it.

Your Assurance

Here is the powerful thing about holiness: holiness does not have a look. Holiness is not hair buns or long skirts. Holiness is not skirts without splits, or clothing that is all white. The devil has many of us fooled into thinking that is what holiness looks like. The enemy has tricked your mind into believing that is why you have not met the standard of holiness. You've been deceived! You think that if you can go ahead and put something on, then God is going to check it off a list. "Be ye all white, for I am all white. Wear ye a long skirt, for I wear a long skirt. Put your hair in a bun, because that is what I told Jesus to do. Jesus walked around with a bun because that's what holiness is." That's exactly what holiness is not!

Holiness is none of that. Holiness is the submission of the soul to the Spirit with the result being a godly life. Holiness means Godlikeness. Jesus Christ epitomized holiness, and He talked to sinners. He went to the wedding in Cana and said, "You are out of wine." He took up for prostitutes, who were seen as unclean, and rehabilitated them. Holiness found its way around dirt. If you consider yourself holy and are only around holy people, then you are not holy. You're the worst kind of fleshy. If Jesus is the epitome of holiness, the icon of holiness, then we need to look at what He did and said, how He acted and moved, and how He engaged others to see what true holiness looks like. Jesus is perfect theology. If we could stop coming up with theology that is outside the life of Jesus Christ, we could come up with trustable theology.

Jesus shows us that even though at times there is an imbalance between grace and truth, they are not at war. There are those who are legalistic, where it's all about truth rules. But when Jesus blends the two, it is not 50/50—it is 100 percent grace and 100 percent truth. Jesus illustrated this when He forgave and accepted the woman who was caught in adultery:

> Jesus stood up and said to her, "Woman, where are they? Has no one condemned you?" She said, "No one, Lord." And Jesus said, "Neither do I condemn you; go, and from now on sin no more."
>
> —John 8:10–11

Jesus wanted her to go forward in the application of the truth based upon the forgiveness that was given. I think we need to come to a balance with both of those worlds—truth and grace—and make sure that it isn't half and half. It must be completely 100 percent grace, 100 percent truth, and that is the replication of Christ Himself.

I'm going to settle the issue on what holiness is using 1 Peter 1:15: "But as he who called you is holy, you also be holy in all your conduct." There is no universal standard of what is appropriate or inappropriate for the most part; it varies from person to person, church to church. There are a number of people with suppressed lust issues who could never go to a village in Ethiopia where a woman does not wear a bra. She has both of her breasts hanging as low as they can get, with a baby on her back—and she loves the Lord and goes to church that way. Is she trying to stir up lust? Is it inappropriate to go into her hut and worship God that way? The answer is no. We have to stop imposing

American ideas on the larger church and church life. What is appropriate or inappropriate varies from culture to culture. There are people who go to church topless in Zambia, and I'm telling you because I know—they go topless, and they serve. There are men who go to churches in Africa with grass skirts. Are they feminine? Do they have a spirit of perversion? No! You might see the same thing in Hawaii. Or what about the kilts men in Scotland wear? If you take your holy self over there and see the men with their bags and their skirts on—and God knows what they'll have on for underwear—is going over there carnal? Is that dressing like the world? The answer is no.

The problem is that most of us only know what we've heard, and so we have not considered how illogical a lot of this stuff is. Are they dressing like the world? No, they are dressing like their culture. This is why we shouldn't put so much emphasis on those things. When we make holiness a size, a color, and a look, the devil says, "Yes. A people will never become what they can't see."

First Peter 1:15 lets us know that if Jesus did not say it, neither should you. It is written "Be ye holy," not "dress ye holy" or "sing ye holy" or "wear thy hair holy." "Be" means that holiness is something to become, not something to do. Holiness is the highest potential of every human heart. Holiness means Godlikeness, not something that is acceptable by a human standard. The highest thing a human being can become is holy because it is seen to be like God. To be holy means to be Godlike in what you do and in what you want. It cannot mean what you dress like, because we don't know where God shops.

Let it Selah a little bit. If dressing differently from the world is such a big issue, then you should use different money than the world uses. You should use different hair products than the world uses. Don't rent your apartment from somebody who is in the world.

Many Christians have double standards. We don't think through these steps. We just say things because we think they sound good—for example, "If you're going to be in a house of God, there ought to be a difference between the people of God and the world." Well, stop going. Don't go to the government to get your SSI or your disability check. Don't let your kids use worldly technology devices; teach them how to read using your Bible. Don't send them to school. It's worldly, it's carnal. Everything in the world is worldly. There should not be a double standard as it relates to clothing and other "worldly" things.

Jesus said, "I do not ask that you take them out of the world, but that you keep them from the evil one" (John 17:15). That was the prayer of Jesus Christ. He prayed that God sanctify us by His truth. God's Word is true. Holiness is the way to power, but it's also about becoming Godlike. No one can become Godlike if they have been judged at the door. The Word of God alone judges people.

Open Access

Many individuals are confused about what "the gospel" is. The gospel is the good news. There are people who say, "I'm called to preach the gospel," and have no idea what they are talking about. The good news is that everybody can have access to deliverance and salvation, not by works, but by faith in Christ, in addition to being baptized in Jesus' name.

Paul stated in Galatians 1:8, "But even if we or an angel from heaven should preach to you a gospel contrary to the one we preached to you, let him be accursed." He continues in verse 10, "For am I now seeking the approval of man, or of God? Or am I trying to please man? If I were still trying to please man, I would not be a servant of Christ."

Your faith should be in God, in what He wants, what He does. Your speech should even sound like Him. Holiness is a change in direction. Anything that is ungodly is of the enemy. Sin is the by-product of a sinful nature, and a sinful nature comes from Satan. That is the reason why you cannot "work" your way into salvation; you must put your faith in the One who has conquered sin, death, and the grave. If you have not received Christ, I encourage you to receive salvation. The Greek word *sōzō* means salvation and freedom from all things—all oppression, poverty, sickness, and disease. But you can't walk into your freedom unless you first accept what Christ has done on the cross. You are incapable of getting rid of a sinful nature—which means you will have no access to walk in deliverance or holiness—outside of the grace of God.

To find this grace, you need Jesus and shepherds to disciple you, because discipleship is also a deliverance issue. Psalm 23:1 states, "The Lord is my shepherd; I shall not want." With God you will lack nothing. Sin comes from lack or a void. Sin is the by-product of needs. The Lord will take you away from that lack. Verses 2–3 of Psalm 23 continue, "He makes me lie down in green pastures. He leads me beside still waters. He restores my soul." The soul cannot be restored outside of this, outside of coming away from need or lack.

Deliverance is both an act and a process. I can speak to something operating in you. I can speak to something operating in your heart, operating in your mind and your will, and it can leave. As you journey with people, you talk to them, and you listen to them, sometimes the strongest bondages are silent. The things that speak up are often the easier things to get out. Going on that journey and developing history with people will allow the layers of the soul to break down. What are these layers called? Barriers to trust. As you develop relationships with people, those trust barriers begin to come down, and you find what is under the layers. Often it is a demon. This is what is identified as the deliverance process: an arrangement to walk out of the known and unknown strongholds into freedom.

Freedom

As I partner with people, places, and the Word, and I continue to grow, I begin to find out that there are things that operate in my soul that I need to be freed from. I've been freed from depression. Some deliverances happen in an instant, such as people being freed from alcoholism, cigarettes, and pornography. However, there are other things that will require walking through the deliverance process in addition to being baptized in Jesus' name and being filled with the Holy Ghost. Yet deliverance will never be successful in a house that is oppressive, under a teaching that is oppressive, and under something that does not give you the right to be free. Holiness is the masterful, beautiful call of God. It is holiness or hell.

Holiness is our aim, and holiness is what I preach. Holiness is what my wife preaches. Holiness is what our church believes. God has put His future for the human race in their pursuit of holiness, and I want to be like Him.

> Beloved, we are God's children now, and what we will be has not yet appeared; but we know that when he appears we shall be like him, because we shall see him as he is.
>
> —1 John 3:2

This is holiness defined. When He appears, we will be like the Son of God. We will think like Him, behave like Him, and want what He wants. We will be motivated by what He is motivated by and refuse to be unlike what He is. That is holiness. It is not a garment, it is a nature. I have taken on the attitudes, the perspectives, the life of Jesus Christ. As Galatians 2:20 says, "The life I now live in the flesh I live by faith in the Son of God, who loved me and gave himself for me." That is a holiness thing. Because it is a nature, there are natural things that you do, and there are things that convict you. There are things that quicken you. For example, because I'm a holy man, if I do something that hurts my wife and I'm not aware of it, I am convicted by the Christ pursuit, the Godlikeness in me, with or without her showing it. I immediately repair and mend it; that's a natural thing. It's not something that is forced; holiness in me wants to do that.

You may realize I'm not afraid of offending people. If you follow me long enough, I'll probably offend you, but it's not with the intent to hurt you. I just have an offensive word and an abrasive gift at times. But if I have offended someone unintentionally, I will get convicted. I will go back to that individual and try to repair it, if possible, to follow peace with all men. I could talk about reasons why people get offended, but the bottom line is, I'm not going to kill myself trying to fix everybody whom I've offended, because some of you need to be offended. The point is that holiness produces natural things in you.

If you were a drug dealer, in your journey to holiness and freedom you begin to stay away from environments that may tempt you or prompt a reaction from your unrenewed nature.

The same is true with people who are coming out of a lifestyle of homosexuality. The same thing is true with people who have been freed from alcoholism and yet their friends still drink. Where the seed of holiness has really been watered, behaviors develop, because Godliness and Godlikeness have seeds that are active. If we run after God, we will walk away from sin. It's about pursuing God and becoming like God.

You can't become godly and still have sin in you. This is very important, because I believe holiness is the word of the day. We just need a bunch of clarity on what it is. I have heard people say, "I came up in a holiness church." What is a church that is not a holiness church? Is there such a thing? Can your church not be a holiness church? Is it a church if it is not holy? What does this mean? Looking at the things that we pride ourselves in proves that we are not as holy as we think, and that we are a bit more arrogant, proud, or self-reliant than we had hoped.

All of this goes together. In summation, acceptance should be present irrespective of appearance. Acceptance is the precursor and the catalyst or the chemical agent that catalyzes deliverance. And deliverance is the act, the journey, and the revelation that prompts holiness. Holiness is where power is produced. You see how that beautiful thing just unbraided. Acceptance is the doorway to deliverance, deliverance is the doorway to holiness, and holiness is the doorway to power. You have no power if you are not holy, you've got talent. Some of you may have witchcraft. Power is born from holiness, holiness is born from deliverance, and deliverance is born from grace. I'm so glad that I serve a "whosoever will" kind of God. I am overjoyed that God is not like His people. I am grateful He won't make YouTube videos. I am thankful He doesn't post shady Facebook statuses.

I am glad that the Lord doesn't even have a Facebook page. People go on social media talking to God as if He is reading their status. It's easier to just pray. I'm grateful God is not like church people. Where in the world would I be? I remember sitting in a crazy home—a literal crazy home—sitting in a rubber row probably about eighteen or nineteen years ago calling out to the God of the church people, and that is not the God that answered. I was so busy feeling guilty about where I was. It was not until He spoke and said, "I am not what you have seen. I am not what they have said. You don't have to be ready for what I want to do. You don't have to be ready for this type of love. You don't have to come out of that rubber jacket for this type of love. You can't even be prepared for it. You don't know." I just yielded to what He wanted to do in that moment, and that is what freed me. He did it!

Shame on those of you that have locked the kingdom because people don't look the part. You are gossiping, venomous, judgmental people. Repent and open the bowls of acceptance and mercy so that the masses can come in. I pray that you take a season to yield to this principle of acceptance. Yield your soul and be renewed in your mind to work out what real holiness is, based upon the Bible. I pray that this has really encouraged you to move forward in a new paradigm, because there is a harvest.